Christmas 1976

this book is given to
ICC Library to convey
appreciation to the
English Department
from a grateful —

WORLD OF CULTURE

THE NOVEL

by Richard Freedman

Newsweek Books, New York

NEWSWEEK BOOKS

Joseph L. Gardner, Editor

Janet Czarnetzki, Art Director
Edwin D. Bayrd, Jr., Associate Editor
Laurie Platt Winfrey, Picture Editor
Kathleen Berger, Copy Editor
Ellen Kavier, Writer-Researcher
Mary Ann Joulwan, Designer

S. Arthur Dembner, President

Frontispiece: Sir Walter Scott's study at Abbotsford

Grateful acknowledgment is made for the use of excerpted material on pages 154–180 from the following works:
Absalom, Absalom! by William Faulkner. Copyright © 1936. Reprinted by permission of Random House, Inc.
Reprinted by permission of Charles Scribner's Sons from *A Farewell to Arms* by Ernest Hemingway. Copyright © 1929 Charles Scribner's Sons.
The Grapes of Wrath by John Steinbeck. Copyright © 1939. Copyright renewed © 1967 by John Steinbeck. Reprinted by permission of The Viking Press, Inc.
A Portrait of the Artist as a Young Man by James Joyce. Copyright © 1964 by the estate of James Joyce, all rights reserved. Reprinted by permission of The Viking Press, Inc.
The Rainbow by D. H. Lawrence. Copyright © 1915 by D. H. Lawrence. Copyright renewed © 1943 by Frieda Lawrence. Reprinted by permission of The Viking Press, Inc.
Reprinted by permission of Charles Scribner's Sons from *Tender Is the Night* by F. Scott Fitzgerald. Copyright 1933, 1934 Charles Scribner's Sons.
Rememberance of Things Past by Marcel Proust. Copyright © 1934. Reprinted by permission of Random House, Inc.

Contents

1

Birth of the Novel

THE ENGLISH NOVEL BEGINS its long and illustrious career in the shady, neatly cultivated garden that one Samuel Richardson has built for his family in the London suburb of Hammersmith. Richardson, a portly, rather pompous man in his late forties, is holding court before the small group of adoring young women seated around him. A veritable "flower garden of ladies," as one biographer will later call them.

It is all very respectable. The girls look up to him as a wise and kind father with whom one can discuss matters that one would rather one's own father didn't know about. Like love affairs. Richardson offers good counsel, and even undertakes to write letters for his fan club—letters to their admirers that catch, better than the girls' own letters could, the precise nuances desired in an eighteenth-century courtship. Richardson has not done much writing before in his busy life, aside from his own business correspondence, some advertising copy for his printing firm, and a curious book called *The Apprentice's Vade Mecum*, in which he dispensed sound advice on matters moral and mercantile to young men anxious to get ahead—as Richardson himself had done—in the business world. However, he is now engaged in writing a book of form letters for all occasions, a volume that he expects to print at a nice profit. One such letter is "From an Uncle to a Nephew, on his keeping bad Company, bad Hours, etc., in his Apprenticeship." Uncles with erring nephews had only to copy out Richardson's letter and fill in the appropriate names. They could be certain that the message would come across loud and clear, as well as wise and elegant.

Letter 138 is from "A Father to a Daughter in Service, on hearing of her Master's attempting her Virtue." As he drafted it, Richardson was reminded of an actual case he had heard about some years earlier, one in which a servant girl withstands the advances of her young master. It occurred to him that the servant girl's story could be told at length in a series of letters—say between the girl and her worried parents miles away—and the resulting book would be both entertaining and instructive, not only to his young ladies but to young people everywhere trying to cope with the problems of love and morality. Within three months the story, *Pamela*, was written, and the English novel was born.

To understand the significance of this event, one must examine two key questions: why was the novel born just then, in 1740, and why to just such an unlikely parent as that stolid master printer, that least

7

The illustration at left, from an early edition of Robinson Crusoe, depicts Daniel Defoe's best-known fictional hero salvaging his belongings from a wrecked ship. Crusoe was to spend twenty-four years on the uninhabited island in the background—and Defoe was to render his everyday existence with an ingenious attention to detail. Precisely because he was so concerned with the surface of life, Defoe failed to impart any information about his characters' deeper feelings and emotional states, one of the basic concerns of the true novel. Nevertheless, he established an important precedent for realistic narrative in English fiction.

"artistic" of temperaments, Samuel Richardson? After all, the Greeks had already invented the novel, producing such classic examples of narrative prose as Longus's *Daphnis and Chloe* as far back as A.D. 250. Medieval prose storytelling had reached a culmination with Boccaccio's wonderful collection of tales, the *Decameron*. Shakespeare's contemporary, Cervantes, had published one of the supreme "novels" of the world—and a highly influential one on future English novelists—*Don Quixote*, in the early seventeenth century. And even in England, Daniel Defoe, some twenty years before Pamela made her debut, was complaining in the preface to his *Moll Flanders* that "The world is so taken up of late with novels and romances."

Part of the problem lies in the terms "novel" and "romance." The word "novel" didn't really come into common use as we understand it until the late eighteenth century, and by then most novelists despised both the word "romance" and the romantic genre. Richardson deliberately avoided what he called "the pomp and parade of romance-writing" as well as "the improbable and marvellous, with which novels generally abound." Yet even he was so impressed by one of the greatest of Elizabethan romances, Sir Philip Sidney's *Arcadia*, that he probably named his own Pamela after a princess in that tale.

On the whole, though, Richardson anchored his fiction not in romance but in the deeply felt reality of his own day and in the virtues of the middle class (romance being essentially an aristocratic genre). In so doing he enabled the novel to hold the proverbial mirror to nature—human nature, really—instead of merely fantasizing about a never-never land stocked with lords and ladies, nymphs and shepherds, part of a misty and largely incredible past. He was perhaps the first to see that the imagination could be applied to contemporary life, that incidents could be invented without seeming unreal.

But aren't Cervantes' and Defoe's novels similarly rooted in the everyday world those authors saw about them? Isn't the very nature of the conflict between illusion and reality the central theme of Cervantes? *Don Quixote* reeks of the Spanish soil, *Moll Flanders* of the rowdy streets of London. Perhaps we could even say that Don Quixote, in his fixation on the remote and romantic past of knight-errantry, could himself represent the authors of most earlier fiction, and that his realistic, earthy companion Sancho Panza is a forecast of the novelist's characteristic attitude since roughly the mid-eighteenth century.

Without being pedantic about the nature of the novel genre itself, most scholars agree that these earlier examples—and there are dozens more—somehow fall short of what they are currently prepared to define as a novel. *Daphnis and Chloe*, like Greek romance in general, is too short. Novels should be of a certain length—although no one will specify just how long. It is also too uncomplicated. The *Decameron* remains a collection of short stories, with almost none of the psychological depth we have come to expect of modern fiction. And the *Arcadia* is totally unconcerned with everyday reality.

Don Quixote poses another sort of problem, for while it inspired a whole genre known as the picaresque novel (which recounts the adventures of a hero who is for one reason or another outside normal society), it is itself perhaps too formally incoherent to be a true novel. That is, no particular adventure of the don and his servant necessarily follows the one which precedes it, or necessarily leads up to the one which follows. Any one adventure is quite interchangeable with any other as far as placement in the book is concerned. Events don't produce inevitable, long-term consequences, as they do in the more carefully wrought novels of our time, and characters are similarly introduced at random, occupy their brief moment on the stage, and then completely disappear.

Defoe's novels offer an even subtler problem. Each of them purports to be the literal truth, merely "edited" by Defoe. *Moll Flanders* is a first-person narrative, presumably written by Moll herself some forty

The father of the English novel, Samuel Richardson (right), was by trade a printer. The moral rectitude that was to manifest itself strongly in Pamela *was also evident in Richardson's first work,* The Apprentice's Vade Mecum. *Just as young ladies were instructed in the rewards of virtue in* Pamela, *so Richardson's manual for young men was a lesson in the rewards of industry. The Hogarth etching seen at left, above, illustrates "The Idle 'Prentice returned from sea and in a garret with a common prostitute," while the one beneath it is entitled "The Industrious 'Prentice grown rich and Sheriff of London."*

years before it was published, and Defoe claims credit only for having cleaned up her language a bit. Why Defoe chose his masks, why he hid behind his characters in a search for absolute, literal reality, is a complicated aesthetic question. But psychologically he seems to have just missed a basic tenet of the novel: that while it usually strives for a sense of reality, it doesn't pretend to be the literal truth. When we read a novel we should be empathizing with the characters and the world they inhabit, but at the same time we should also be aware that we are reading a fiction that has its own higher truths to relate.

Defoe, an experienced newspaperman, blurred that borderline between journalistic factuality and artistic truth. In addition, his narratives tend to sprawl. He was clearly making them up as he went along, with little idea of where they would end, or why any particular incident should occur where it does rather than someplace else in the story. We will see Dickens and serial novelists in general operating in this manner in the nineteenth century, but Dickens, at least, had a better

11

instinctive sense of form than had Defoe. For one thing, he had read more novels—including Defoe's.

Worst of all, perhaps, Defoe was so concerned with the vivid rendering of the surface of life—which he does supremely well—that he seems to have had little time, patience, or talent for a deeper exploration of his characters' inner psychological and spiritual lives. Robinson Crusoe on his desert island behaves just the way he would behave back in England; Defoe was more interested in his material survival than in his mental survival—and what must have been the extremely trying psychological trauma of complete loneliness, alienation, and abandonment is barely touched on.

With *Pamela*, though, we have something completely different. How aware was Richardson of himself as an innovator? He did write a friend that he hoped his novel "might introduce a new species of writing." And here indeed was a coherent, if somewhat prolix, plot, one with a good deal of suspense, about the fortunes of a girl with whom many eighteenth-century readers could identify. Richardson had a keen sense of the class system of his day. He knew how many servant girls secretly aspired to marry their masters, how unlikely this was, just what the pitfalls were, and what the attitudes of society would be toward such a misalliance.

In addition to his personal genius, Richardson had the luck of writing at a time when there was an almost wholly new audience for his works, a new reading public. The first circulating library in London was established in 1740, the year *Pamela* was published, and circulating libraries were to have a profound effect, albeit sometimes an unhealthy one, on the kinds of novels Englishmen would produce for the next one hundred and fifty years. There was a new middle-class audience of sufficient leisure and literacy to want, and be able to read, novels about themselves and their world. Cheaper printing methods, improved postal service, and an increasing population—London's doubled during the eighteenth century—all contributed to the rise of the novel.

Futhermore, the religious quarrels of the seventeenth century were over, and reader interest in theological controversy waned accordingly during the eighteenth century. Where before the average Englishman's library consisted of a Bible, the collected works of Shakespeare, a *Pilgrim's Progress* or *Paradise Lost*, and the bound sermons of the local minister, it now included a newspaper like Addison and Steele's *Tatler* or *Spectator* and perhaps a novel or two as well. And who would read a collection of sermons when he could read a tense, suspenseful, racy story like *Pamela*? In important ways, the novel got started as a secular replacement for the religious literature of the previous century. In Fielding's *Joseph Andrews*, for instance, we laugh at the attempts of the hapless Parson Adams to hawk his collected sermons to a bookseller; clearly the market was dead for that sort of literary goods in the Age of Reason.

The market was vibrantly alive for *Pamela*, however, and Richardson's work was an immediate sensation not merely among ambitious servant girls in England but among philosophers in France. One of them, the Encyclopedist Diderot, no mean novelist himself, ranked

"Virtue Rewarded" was the subtitle Richardson gave his epistolary novel Pamela—his chaste heroine's recompense being marriage to her former employer, Mr. B (above, right). Previous to the wedding, Mr. B. is portrayed as a lascivious brute who pursues Pamela with intentions that are far from honorable (above, left). Pamela refuses to submit, however, and at their nuptials Mr. B. is transformed into the ideal mate.

Richardson with Moses, Sophocles, and Euripides; and in 1744 Benjamin Franklin printed *Pamela* in Philadelphia, making it the first novel to be published in the American colonies.

Not everyone was so taken with the book, however. Many parodies appeared, most notably an anonymous one called *Shamela* that turned out to be the work of Henry Fielding, who was on the verge of beginning his own career as a novelist and who became Richardson's ideological opponent and chief rival. Richardson called *Shamela* a "lewd and ungenerous engraftment" upon his *Pamela*, and the reasons for his pique are perfectly—and hilariously—obvious to anyone who reads Fielding's parody.

What annoyed Fielding was what he considered the false morality

of *Pamela*. Richardson had set up a poor but fanatically virtuous heroine who spends the first two-thirds of the book desperately escaping the clutches of her lascivious master, Mr. B. When she finally manages to inveigle him into marriage as the price of her chastity, all is happy, and the man whom she had always thought of as a brute and a scoundrel is revealed to be an ideal husband. Richardson gave fair warning in his subtitle, "Virtue Rewarded," but Fielding wondered about the ambiguous morality of Pamela's marrying the man who had so tormented her, and he sensed that under the cover of telling a highly moral tale Richardson was in fact indulging in his own lubricious fantasies, an insight repeated in our time by D. H. Lawrence, who said that "Boccaccio at his hottest seems to me less pornographical than *Pamela*."

Within the brief, farcical scope of *Shamela*, Fielding completely turned the tables, making his heroine an admitted prostitute who single-mindedly dupes her innocent master into marriage.

Fielding, eighteen years Richardson's junior, no more consciously set out to be a novelist than Richardson had done. Indeed, we will find all the supreme masters of the eighteenth-century English novel coming to fiction writing almost by chance, and from very different professional backgrounds. Defoe was a businessman and journalist, Richardson a printer, Smollett a physician, and Sterne a minister. Fielding began as a dramatist, producing some twenty-five highly successful but lightweight farces and bawdy burlesques for the London stage before the repressive Theatrical Licensing Act of 1737 put an end to that career. Then, with characteristic aplomb, he began a second career—as a lawyer —and was called to the bar just a few months before *Pamela* was published. Ultimately he became a distinguished jurist, rising to the rank of magistrate for Middlesex County and developing a plan for the first serious professional police force in London.

It was just at the onset of his legal career, however, that Fielding became so obsessed with *Pamela* that he decided his own *Shamela* was not enough. He began yet another parody, *Joseph Andrews*, but after writing only a few chapters he tired of flailing Richardson and took off on his own, creating his first genuine novel—or as he called it, "a comic epic-poem in prose." From this description, and from the important theoretical preface he wrote to *Joseph Andrews*, it is clear that Fielding was aware he was creating an essentially new genre, and, as a much better-educated man than Richardson, was trying to find antecedents for it in such classical forms as the epic and the drama.

Joseph Andrews was most deeply influenced, however, not by the classics of antiquity but by *Don Quixote*. The true hero is not Pamela Andrews's absurdly chaste brother, Joseph, but Parson Adams, idealistic and unworldly like Cervantes' don, who travels about England in meandering, picaresque fashion, meeting a variety of adventures (usually comically disastrous) at inns and along the rough highways of a preindustrial society.

While Fielding was inventing a new mode for the English novel, Richardson was hardly lying fallow. *Pamela* was succeeded in 1748 by his masterpiece, the million-word *Clarissa*, which was also a novel-in-letters, or epistolary novel, and also about a damsel in distress. In other respects, however, *Clarissa* was no more like *Pamela* than *Hamlet* is like *The Comedy of Errors*, for Richardson had matured immensely as an artist. Where *Pamela* consisted essentially of only one set of correspondence—that between Pamela and her worried parents—*Clarissa* was comprised of several sets, most notably between Clarissa and her confidante, Anna Howe, and between Clarissa's dangerous lover, Lovelace, and his friend John Belford. Thus Richardson was able to coun-

In the portrait at right, Henry Fielding's multifaceted career is represented by theater masks and law books in addition to novels. The British novelist began his literary career writing farces and satires for the London stage, but he was forced to seek another vocation after passage of a repressive licensing act. Undaunted, he studied law and became a prominent magistrate. His satiric gifts were to resurface in Shamela, *his parody of* Pamela, *and reach fruition in* Joseph Andrews *and* Tom Jones. *At left above are several scenes from the latter, a sprawling picaresque novel whose lusty but essentially benevolent hero must learn to be prudent.*

terpoint his plot with all the complexity of a Bach fugue; the same incident would be seen through different eyes, each bringing its own subjective vision to bear on it and leading to a philosophical relativism, a hopeless searching for the chimera of objective truth, astonishing for the eighteenth century but most relevant to the twentieth, as the novels of Proust and Durrell—and such movies as Kurosawa's *Rashomon*—would demonstrate.

Even Fielding had to recognize that *Clarissa* was a masterpiece, and handsomely admitted as much in a recently discovered letter to Richardson that has upset many standard theories about the direct antipathy between the two novelists. Yet the central story of *Clarissa*, a middle-class girl who spurns her parents' odious choice of a suitor and runs off with the dashing, cavalier Lovelace only to be immured in a brothel, drugged, raped, and finally left to die tragically and heroically, still upset Fielding's sense of values. Did it really necessarily follow that a girl who left home must be ruined? Fielding himself had eloped with his wife Charlotte in 1734, and they had lived happily ever after—at least until her death a decade later, whereupon Fielding imitated the protagonist of another Richardson novel by marrying his late wife's servant girl, Mary Daniel.

So in 1749 Fielding answered Richardson's masterpiece, *Clarissa*, with his own masterpiece, *Tom Jones*. Here the heroine, Sophia Western, closely modeled on Fielding's first wife, leaves her bullying father —as Clarissa had done—to pursue her errant, seemingly amoral lover, Tom. But this time all ends happily. The villains of *Tom Jones* exhibit the hypocritical surface morality Fielding felt Richardson was preaching, but they are all deeply corrupt within. Tom, the scapegrace hero, must indeed learn to be more prudent in order to get along in the world, but his sins are venial in Fielding's eyes because they stem from a lusty but basically benevolent heart. Tom, unlike Richardson's Lovelace, is redeemable; the sex urge, Fielding seems to say, need not necessarily end in social and moral disaster.

Indeed, over a century later Thackeray would complain that Fielding had been the last English novelist "to be able to describe a man" in all his aspects, including the sexual. Modern readers may question, though, whether for all his charm and high spirits, for all his urbane wit and mastery of form, Fielding had indeed probed the depths of his hero as profoundly as Richardson had probed the inner psyche of Clarissa.

Nearly everyone agrees that *Tom Jones* is a perfectly plotted novel, Coleridge going so far as to say its plot was one of the three "most perfect" ever planned in all literature (the other two being Sophocles' *Oedipus Tyrannus* and Ben Jonson's *The Alchemist*). The massive novel is organized into eighteen books, evenly divided in groups of six, and overall resembles a giant three-act play. Fielding's experience in the theater obviously equipped him very well for imposing a kind of dramatic order on an otherwise sprawling picaresque plot. Other critics, notably Dr. Johnson and Jane Austen, were a good deal less enthusiastic, distrusting the implications of Fielding's easygoing approach to morality and seeing in Richardson's puritanism a considerably more reliable guide to human conduct.

Tobias Smollett (above) drew on his own experience as a surgeon's mate to limn the memorable naval passages in Roderick Random *and* Peregrine Pickle *(below). A physician by training, he was appalled by eighteenth-century England's reliance on quack doctors, whom he was to caricature as devastatingly as did Hogarth (opposite).*

Fielding himself seems to have come to some realization that the world was a more dangerous place than he had pictured it in *Joseph Andrews* and *Tom Jones*. In his last novel, *Amelia*, the wit has given way to a somber account of London criminal life, influenced no doubt by Fielding's years on the bench. It is filled with the grave compassion that apparently characterized Fielding's attitude as a magistrate, and on the whole makes a sad pendant to a glittering career.

Similarly, Richardson's career ended on a muted note. In his last novel, *Sir Charles Grandison*, he tackled the almost impossible task of portraying a good man, and like other writers before and after him discovered that most readers prefer following the dangerous antics of villains to the prosy sermonizing of an overgrown Boy Scout. A virtuous woman sorely tested, like Pamela or Clarissa, may excite empathy and suspense; Richardson's Sir Charles is merely a priggish bore. In the novel, at least, virtue must be its own reward, for undiluted, untested virtue makes for very unrewarding reading.

The two other major English novelists of the eighteenth century, Tobias Smollett and Laurence Sterne, were less concerned with the conflict between vice and virtue than Richardson and Fielding had been. Smollett, a Scotsman with a medical degree from the University of Glasgow, was only twenty when he served as surgeon's mate aboard H.M.S. *Chichester* during the ill-fated Cartagena expedition of 1741.

There he became aware of the privations and injustices suffered by his fellow seamen, and there his keen intelligence was aroused by the stupid blundering of the admiralty brass. Settling down in London as a spectacularly unsuccessful physician, Smollett turned his hand to writing, and in 1748, the year Richardson produced *Clarissa*, he published his first picaresque novel, *Roderick Random*.

Both *Roderick Random* and its successor, *Peregrine Pickle*, are extremely loose narratives in which the interest is sustained by the vigor of Smollett's prose and, above all, by the naval passages. Roderick Random finds himself aboard a warship and undergoes essentially Smollett's experiences, and the most memorable character in *Peregrine Pickle* is not the hero, but a retired old salt, Commodore Hawser Trun-

The bold literary experimentation of Laurence Sterne (left), whose novel Tristram Shandy *was published in the 1760's, went unmatched until the publication of James Joyce's* Ulysses *in the 1920's. Although the work was scoffed at by Dr. Johnson and Samuel Richardson, it proved to be enormously popular—and it firmly established the obscure Irish clergyman's literary reputation.* Tristram Shandy *is indeed unique. A purported biography, it never gets beyond the second or third year of the protagonist's life and is sprinkled with random reflections on almost everything under the sun. It also abounds in typographical eccentricities—dots, dashes, asterisks, one-sentence-long chapters, blank pages, and unfinished sentences.*

nion, whose maladjustment to the landlubber's life is a source of high comedy in the novel. In a sense, Smollett may be said to have invented the English sea novel, giving rise not only to the once-popular Captain Marryat, but to the far more important Joseph Conrad.

It was not until 1771, the year of his death, that Smollett achieved his masterpiece, *Humphry Clinker*, which combines the picaresque with the epistolary novel in a remarkable way. The characters journey aimlessly about England and Scotland, as in picaresque fiction, but their adventures are told in a series of eighty-two letters, counterpointed as Richardson had done in *Clarissa* to show their varying responses to one another and to the places they visit. Thus the real hero of the novel, the cantankerous but basically good-hearted Matthew Bramble, responds angrily to the sordidness of such places as Bath and London, while his romantic niece Lydia finds only excitement in the vivid social scenes. Smollett, as a physician, was appalled by the utter lack of sanitation and the pandemic reliance on quacks he found in mid-eighteenth-century England, and *Humphry Clinker* abounds in lurid descriptions of disease that can still appall the squeamish reader.

Far less urbane than Fielding, and with a larger streak of coarseness in his makeup, Smollett gives, among other things, an unparalleled picture of English lowlife that has endured to this day. In one of his characters, the semiliterate serving girl Win Jenkins, he also manages to anticipate the complex punning technique of James Joyce. It is Win who writes the last letter in the book, and in it she describes a triple wedding ceremony thus: "We were yesterday three kiple chined, by the grease of God, in the holy bands of matter-money"—and suddenly we are in the richly allusive, densely textured verbal world of *Finnegans Wake*. *Humphry Clinker* is a wiser, mellower, and better-humored novel than Smollett's rather raw earlier works, but its ribald high spirits have offended many a reader in the two centuries since its initial publication.

Even more ribald, and more influential on the modern novel, was *Tristram Shandy* (1760–67), the masterpiece of an eccentric Irish clergyman named Laurence Sterne. It is one of the peculiar glories of the English novel that no sooner had it been born than it produced an anti-novel. For in *Tristram Shandy* Sterne plays in the most sophisticated ways possible with such metaphysical assumptions of the novel as its relationship to "real" reality, its dependence on a hero or heroine, and its need for coherent, chronological plot development.

Sterne seems to have tossed all these conventions into an electric fan and then reassembled them willy-nilly. His idiosyncratic handling of time, his narrative process involving seemingly random, disgressive thought associations, and the innumerable verbal and even typographical tricks he plays on his readers were all to have profound influence on such modernists as Joyce and Borges. For all its scatterbrained surface, *Tristram Shandy* is a monument of aesthetic and philosophical speculation about the nature and scope of the novel.

Yet a short time after the last volume was published, Dr. Johnson proclaimed: "Nothing odd will do long: *Tristram Shandy* did not last." For once the good doctor was wrong, if, as usual when he erred, for the right reasons. *Tristram Shandy* is so odd that while it has attracted devoted partisans over the years, at least as many readers have been simply repelled by its antinovelistic antics. It seems wholly outside the mainstream of fiction; a biological sport in a way, and yet it is an immensely attractive one to readers prepared to follow the odd twistings and turnings of Sterne's fancy—at once leering and sentimental, jesting and philosophical—rather than being put off by the palpable lack of coherent plot. And beneath the deliberately eccentric surface of *Tristram Shandy* there lurk some fairly standard character types, instantly recognizable to any reader of eighteenth-century English novels; it is just the way in which they are rendered that makes *Tristram Shandy* so unique.

But if *Tristram Shandy* is *sui generis*, the years during which it was written also saw the beginning of a genre that has been almost too pro-

When Horace Walpole (left, above) reconstructed his mansion Strawberry Hill (below, left) in the Gothic style, he initiated an important trend in English architecture. Similarly, his Castle of Otranto *marks the genesis of the Gothic novel. In the wistful portrait at right, Mary Wollstonecraft Shelley actually resembles a Gothic heroine. Her first novel,* Frankenstein, *has endured as one of the genre's few masterpieces.*

lific right up to the present day. This is the so-called Gothic novel, invented by Horace Walpole in 1764 with the publication of *The Castle of Otranto*. Walpole was the son of Sir Robert Walpole, one of the most influential—and most hated—of eighteenth-century prime ministers, a man pilloried by Fielding in *Jonathan Wild*. Young Walpole, who never became the power in politics his father had been, was a rather effeminate dilettante and connoisseur whose masterpiece, perhaps, is not a novel but a fake Gothic mansion, Strawberry Hill, which he spent twenty years and a considerable fortune remodeling and furbishing to his somewhat exotic tastes.

Walpole was a prolific correspondent whose letters, a splendid compendium of court gossip now being published in their entirety for the first time, will eventually fill fifty huge volumes. *The Castle of Otranto* was his only venture in fiction. It is in every way an amateurish performance, yet somehow Walpole managed to hit on the themes, atmosphere, tone, and even props that would later accompany Gothic fiction. Like many pioneer works, *The Castle of Otranto* is itself crude, however, and almost unreadable today except for unintended laughs.

Walpole said the crucial vision of his novel came to him in a dream, and to a certain extent all Gothic fiction is dreamlike, or, more precisely, nightmarish. It appeared in the mid-1700's as an escape from the rationality of the High Augustan world of Pope and Johnson; an unleashing, in Freudian terms, of the long suppressed id, and is perhaps best approached by psychoanalytic, rather than literary, criticism.

Typically, the eighteenth-century Gothic novel, as practiced not only by Walpole but by such followers as Ann Radcliffe (*The Mysteries of Udolpho*), Charles Maturin (*Melmoth the Wanderer*), and Matthew Lewis (*The Monk*), deals with a terrified English Protestant virgin in the clutches of a quasi-satanic Catholic hero-villain, at once attractive and menacing, who usually lives in somber, isolated splendor in Italy. Clearly, subconscious sexual, national, and religious fears are being exploited in Gothic fiction, often so subconsciously that the author himself is unfortunately unaware of their significance. Classically the heroine is scared out of her wits by the supernatural goings-on in the hero-villain's castle: family portraits that groan and bleed, trap-doors leading to musty dungeons, mysterious rooms to which she is forbidden access, caskets opening in the dead of night.

It's all good, dirty fun, of more psychohistoric than purely literary significance. Rapidly it became a stereotyped convention with two possible denouements: either there is a rational explanation for the supernatural effects (they have been specially rigged and staged by the hero-villain to frighten the heroine into signing some document that will benefit him) or, more suggestively, the reader is left with an ambiguous sense of all-pervasive evil, of more things in heaven and earth than are dreamed of in our philosophies—especially if we are eighteenth-century rationalists.

For at the time, the Gothic novel, like its sister the Oriental tale—*Vathek* by William Beckford, an even more eccentric dilettante than Walpole, is a good example of the latter—provided a healthy release for the subconscious, too long pent up in the culture of the eighteenth century. A precursor of romanticism, the genre occasionally threw up a masterpiece such as Mary Wollstonecraft Shelley's *Frankenstein*, which has haunted the folk consciousness ever since. In the nineteenth century some of its elements entered the more serious and sophisticated fiction of the Brontë sisters, Dickens, and Wilkie Collins. Alas, most of the products of the Gothic imagination, from Walpole to the countless mass-produced paperbacks filling the "Gothic" racks of modern drugstores and card shops, have been unmitigated trash, designed to give the naïve and nervous a good frisson of terror, and then to be forgotten.

One avid reader of Gothics who was neither naïve nor nervous, and who began her most distinguished literary career with a spoof of the genre, was Jane Austen. The daughter of a country clergyman, Jane Austen was born in 1775, at the time of the American Revolution, and died in 1817, two years after Waterloo. Her life span, then, includes forty-two of the most hectic and dramatic years in English history, yet such is the nature of her serene art that one would hardly guess it was being produced against a backdrop of heroic struggle.

Rather, Austen, living the quiet life of a middle-class provincial spinster, was an instinctively self-limiting artist who, in circumscribing her scope, as she said, to "3 or 4 Families in a Country Village," managed to bring a new depth and maturity to the English novel. Not for

Pride and Prejudice *(above) remains Jane Austen's best-known work, and that novel's heroine, Elizabeth Bennet, is still among the most admired figures in English literature. Although not published until 1813,* Pride and Prejudice *was written in 1797 when its author was only twenty-two years old. As with her other novels, Austen here limits herself to describing that which she knew first-hand—"3 or 4 Families in a Country Village." Precisely because her scope is narrow, her focus is sharp and clear.*

her were the febrile fantasies of the Gothic novel, although she seems to have read them all with considerable pleasure. She seems equally untouched by the romantic revolution raging about her in the other arts, and by the products of the American and French revolutions, which were radically altering the world she lived in. Instead, she is clearly rooted in the earlier eighteenth-century world; her gods are Richardson, Dr. Johnson, and Common Sense.

Thus *Northanger Abbey*, probably her first mature novel (dating the composition of Austen's novels is still a vexed issue), begins as a spoof of the Gothic genre, in much the same way that Fielding's *Joseph Andrews* began as a parody of *Pamela*. Catherine Morland, the antiheroine, is plain, gawky, and not overbright. When she is invited to the home of a young man she has fallen in love with, she fantasizes that his father has long ago done away with his mother, and that all sorts of spooks from the past haunt the place. When the truth is finally revealed to her she comes to understand that people in real life can be infinitely more terrifying than anything the Gothic imagination can produce.

In a sense, all six of Jane Austen's mature novels deal with the education of the heroine. Marianne Dashwood in *Sense and Sensibility* must learn to curb her romantic sensitivity in order to cope maturely with the exigencies of real love. Emma Woodhouse, in *Emma*, must learn to stop manipulating the lives of others in her passion for matchmaking. And Elizabeth Bennet of *Pride and Prejudice*, perhaps the most delectable heroine in English fiction, must learn to judge people by the reality underlying their surfaces.

Jane Austen herself spoke of "the little bit (two inches wide) of ivory on which I work with so fine a brush, as to produce little effect, after much labour," and she confessed herself to the prince regent's librarian, who was after her to produce either a sentimental romance about a clergyman or a magniloquent historical novel, as "the most unlearned and uninformed female who ever dared to be an authoress."

Her sense of her own limitations can trick us, however, into failing to realize how profound she is within them. Because she was never present when men were talking to one another without women around, there is no scene in any of her novels of a purely masculine conversation. Women talk to women and to men, but men never speak only to men. Yet such is her skill that this omission is never felt, and her male characters, based purely on external observation in mixed society, are wholly convincing. Despite the fact that two of her brothers were naval officers during the Napoleonic Wars, there is no sense in her novels that England is not at peace, although in her last novel, *Persuasion*, the hero is a naval captain. Austen did not trust her imagination to render scenes to which she had no personal access as fully and concretely as she wished, and so is supremely the novelist who writes about what she knows at first hand. Although the world she writes about is limited to long visits with country neighbors, to cozy gossip and matchmaking, this world is rendered with a depth which has often, and rightly, been called Shakespearian.

Another unfair criticism frequently made of Jane Austen is that essentially she kept rewriting the same novel. It is true that the court-

ship and eventual marriage of hero and heroine and their coming to terms with the society in which they live form the skeleton of all her novels, yet each has its own individual tone and characteristics. On the whole, the earlier novels—*Northanger Abbey, Sense and Sensibility,* and *Pride and Prejudice*—are wittier and more high-spirited than the later ones—*Emma, Mansfield Park,* and *Persuasion*. The latter two particularly are almost grave and border on tragedy, although the great Austen wit is never entirely suppressed. In *Persuasion*, she even seems to be coming to terms with romanticism, and it is fascinating, if frustrating, to speculate where Austen's art might have gone had she not died so young.

As it is, her six novels, which brought her little fame and less fortune in her lifetime, have endured as one of the highest peaks in the mountain range of English fiction. She is really the first consummate artist in the English novel, an artist whose technique is always assured and whose vision of the social world is never less than profound.

2

"The Great Form"

ONE OF THE FEW READERS sufficiently acute to recognize the quiet greatness of Jane Austen during her lifetime was Sir Walter Scott—whose
contemporary review of *Emma* is a tribute to both his catholicity of
taste and generosity of spirit, for Scott was in almost every way Austen's polar opposite. Where Austen wrote profoundly within a deliberately narrow social scope, Scott ranged widely over nearly the entire
spectrum of European history. He was, however, shallower in his conception of character, less realistic in his handling of dialogue, often
slapdash in style, and as a consequence he is nowadays more admired
than he is read.

Today it is almost impossible to gauge the immense vogue Scott
enjoyed during his lifetime. He was by far the most popular novelist up
to his time, and his vast readership was to be surpassed, among novelists
writing in English, only by Dickens. So revered was he in the American South before the Civil War, for instance, that Mark Twain only
half-jestingly accused him of causing the war through the sheer impact
that his concepts of chivalry exerted on the minds of the southern,
plantation-owning class.

This son of a middle-class Edinburgh lawyer, although suffering
from the effects of a childhood bout of poliomyelitis, nevertheless made
enough money by 1811, the year he turned forty, to purchase Abbotsford, a grandiose, baronial Gothic pile near the Scottish-English border.
And this was before he had even begun to write novels, for Scott first
gained worldwide fame as a collector of Scottish ballads and min-
strelsy. Then, turning to poetry, he awakened the romantic imagination
of Europe to the glamour of the Scottish past in such original narrative
poems as *The Lay of the Last Minstrel* and *The Lady of the Lake*.

When Lord Byron exploded on the literary scene in 1812 with the
first two cantos of *Childe Harold's Pilgrimage*, Scott saw himself out-
done in the poetic field by this even more glamorous rival. He therefore turned to fiction, publishing *Waverley* in 1814. Characteristically,
he did so anonymously, as fiction still had a somewhat disreputable
air about it. Scott once referred to himself as "The Great Unknown,"
for while his novels sold prodigiously, they did not bear his name until
much later in his career.

Scott's thirty-odd novels fall into two basic classes: those dealing
with Scottish history of the seventeenth and eighteenth centuries—stir-

"The Wizard of the North," Sir Walter Scott, used Scotland's heroic past as material for many of his novels. Though not the first to write historical novels, he was a master of the genre, immensely prolific and enor- mously successful. By the time he was forty, Scott had earned enough money to build Abbots- ford (opposite), his beloved estate on the banks of the Tweed.

27

ring and troubled times North of the Border—and those ranging further afield in European history, usually into the Middle Ages. The former —*The Heart of Midlothian* and *Old Morality* are good examples—are generally the more successful as works of art. The overpraised *Ivanhoe* is an example of the latter genre.

Scott brought several gifts to the writing of fiction. He could populate a large canvas, could work up considerable narrative drive, had a subtle moral sense, and understood Scottish history profoundly and sympathetically. However, his characters tend to be stagy and stereotyped, his dialogue is often excruciatingly pompous and overblown, his situations sentimental or melodramatic. He is at his best with Scottish peasant types, who speak a colorful, pithy dialect that is difficult for non-Scots to read but worth the effort.

To his initial readers, Scott's allure lay in his dramatization and glamorization of history and the high moral precepts that governed both his life and his fiction. He helped make fiction respectable, and he created the historical novel practically single-handedly—with profound effects on such diverse talents as James Fenimore Cooper in the United States, Alessandro Manzoni in Italy, Victor Hugo in France, and Leo Tolstoy in Russia. But Scott wrote far too much far too quickly. When the publishing firm of Ballantyne, in which he had an interest, collapsed in the financial panic of 1826, Scott spent the last six years of his life in a fury of creation, determined that no creditor should lose a penny because of him. He also refused to part with Abbotsford, his beloved white elephant of a home. The pace of production killed him, and honorable as his behavior was it must be said that his later fiction suffered as a result.

Recently there have been signs of a Scott revival, but it is doubtful if he will ever regain the glory he once enjoyed as Britain's supreme romantic novelist. That role is now occupied by the Brontë sisters, the mysterious appeal of whose lives almost, but not quite, overshadows the purely literary power of their masterpieces, *Jane Eyre*, *Villette*, and *Wuthering Heights*. To understand the place the Brontë sisters occupy in English fiction one must realize that when the full flood of romanticism hit England toward the end of the eighteenth century, it expressed itself most powerfully in poetry. When we think of English romanticism we immediately think of Blake, Wordsworth, Coleridge, Keats, Shelley, and Byron. Aside from Scott and some minor Gothic novelists —and always the supremely classical Jane Austen—the high romantic period was not a very fruitful one for the novel. Well after the tide had ebbed, however, the Brontës produced at least two romantic masterworks in fiction that are worthy to stand with the finest poetry of Keats and Shelley.

The daughters of a highly eccentric Irish clergyman, the Reverend Patrick Brontë, Charlotte and Emily grew up in Haworth parsonage on the remote, forbidding, windswept Yorkshire moors. For company they had only their sisters Maria, Elizabeth, and Anne and their brother Branwell. Maria and Elizabeth died of the family disease, tuberculosis, while still schoolgirls at the Cowan Bridge School, a place Charlotte later bitterly caricatured as Lowood in *Jane Eyre*. Charlotte and Emily,

Sir Walter Scott (opposite) was immensely popular during his lifetime. His imaginative, colorful works, filled with the pageantry of Scotland's past, satisfied romantic appetites that had been whetted by Gothic novels and inflamed by the poetry of Wordsworth, Shelley, and Byron. But huge debts, in part incurred at Abbotsford (above), caused Scott to write too much too quickly. Both his later work and his health suffered from the frantic pace he set for himself.

who were also supposed to attend the school, were withdrawn on their sisters' deaths.

One day in June of 1826 Mr. Brontë brought home a box of wooden soldiers. The surviving children shared them and wove around them a fantasy world about which they began writing stories and poems. Charlotte and Branwell were in charge of the imaginary kingdom of Angria; Emily and Anne, of the rival Gondal. Not much survives of the juvenilia they composed about these fantasy lands, but the little we have is enough to attest to the high imaginative powers of the children and to the great poetic gifts of Emily in particular. Many of the poems she composed for the Gondal saga foreshadow themes that she was later to develop more fully in *Wuthering Heights*.

In 1844 Charlotte and Emily went to Brussels to improve their French prior to setting up a school of their own at home. They stayed at a pension run by one Constantin Héger, a married pedagogue with whom Charlotte fell in love. This frustrated love was to bear fruit in her first novel, *The Professor*, and she was to return to it at the end of her life in her last and far stronger novel, *Villette*.

In 1846 the three surviving sisters published a curious volume called *Poems, by Currer, Ellis and Acton Bell.* Currer was Charlotte; Ellis, Emily; and Acton, Anne. The book sold two copies. Similarly stillborn was an attempt to set up "The Misses Brontë's Establishment for the Board and Education of a Limited Number of Young Ladies." It was so limited that not one pupil signed up. Undeterred, the sisters worked on their novels. Charlotte completed *The Professor*; Anne, *Agnes Grey*; and Emily, at twenty-eight the eldest and most astonishingly accomplished, *Wuthering Heights.* By 1847 these novels were all in print, as was Charlotte's *Jane Eyre.* By the next year, Emily was dead and brother Branwell, a talented artist, had destroyed himself with drugs and drink. Then in 1849 Anne, the weakest novelist of the sisters, also died, leaving Charlotte alone to cope with her increasingly difficult father, to reach some measure of fame in literary London, to marry a clergyman in 1854, and to die nine months later, aged thirty-nine, while expecting a child.

The seemingly haunted lives of the Brontë sisters should not distract attention from what is most important about them—their art. The great mystery here is how Charlotte and Emily in particular were able to rise to such heights of fiction at such a young age and with so little contact with the outside world. To be sure they must have led a rich fantasy life, and they clearly did much reading in their remote parsonage, but neither *Jane Eyre* nor *Wuthering Heights* seems in any way bookish or the product of a mind immature either in the production of fiction or in knowledge of humanity.

Of the two, *Jane Eyre* is the more conventional, masterpiece though it is; if Charlotte had lived longer she might well have become a fairly standard writer of Victorian fiction. As it is, *Jane Eyre*, for all its traditionally Gothic elements—hero-villain Rochester, his mad wife immured in an attic room, Jane's Cinderella girlhood culminating in a happy marriage to a social superior—nevertheless pulsates with genuine emotion, a deep perception of human nature, and a felt reality that have kept it alive to the present day.

By far the more remarkable novel is Emily's *Wuthering Heights*, which seems not so much a novel as a great romantic poem, one that many critics have rightly seen as being on a level with *King Lear.* Its storm-tossed passions are kept rigorously in check by an extraordinary tightness of construction that involves using two narrators and a series of complex time shifts. Emily Brontë somehow imposed form on the chaotic emotions she unleashed with an inborn sophistication about the possibilities of narrative that was far ahead of her time. Only the novels of Henry James and Joseph Conrad, or F. Scott Fitzgerald's *The Great Gatsby*—all much later works—show comparable skill in coping with the chronological and narrative problems that Emily instinctively set herself and solved with great brilliance. In this, as well as in other ways, *Wuthering Heights* is almost a throwback in English fiction, and although it was published a decade after Victoria became queen, it seems totally out of place as a Victorian novel, harking back, rather, to the great romantic poets.

For what sticks in the mind long after we have finished it is not a

The imaginative gifts of all three of the Brontë sisters were extraordinary. Their lives in the remote parsonage at Haworth, hemmed-in by the barren moors of Yorkshire (below), were bleak and circumscribed. They therefore escaped into fantasy—and into their art.

broad cast of characters, usually caricatured and one-dimensional, or a rich social scene, or a series of ingeniously interwoven plots, but rather an aura, an atmosphere, a metaphysical questioning of man's place in the universe. We remember Catherine Earnshaw and Heathcliff calling to each other on the barren moors, a love both transcendent and deeply destructive, written about with a combination of emotional fervor and mature intelligence practically unique in the English novel. It is both a

profound questioning and a passionate affirmation of romantic ideals; a cool critique of romantic egoism that nevertheless draws its very life and spirit from its highly romantic attitudes toward such subjects as nature, love, and death.

By the 1840's a mode of novel production had arisen that seriously altered the nature of the English novel and that had no place for such lonely flukes of fiction as *Wuthering Heights*. This was the method of serial publication by which a novel would appear in monthly installments over a period of a year to eighteen months. Each installment would carry three or four chapters and would sell for a shilling. Then, when the serial had run its course, one could either have the installments bound into book form or purchase the completed work in a bound, three-volume set. The installments themselves did not necessarily appear in magazines, as novels today are sometimes serialized, but in individual paperbound form, usually bearing two to four illustrations per issue and some advertising matter on the back cover. This method of novel publication, going hand-in-hand with the burgeoning growth of a system of private lending libraries across Britain, had a profound impact on the nature of the Victorian novel. Dickens, Thackeray, George Eliot, and Trollope all wrote at least some serial novels, and in Dickens's case in particular, this publishing process governed his art to an incalculable extent.

The first thing to realize about serial publication is that more often than not the novelist was creating his work as it was appearing before the public; unlike today's serialization of fiction, it was not merely a matter of chopping up an already finished novel into installments. This of course placed an immense burden on the novelist, and few novelists apart from Dickens had the prodigality of imagination, the facility of style, and the boundless capacity for work necessary to bring off such a method of writing and publishing.

Dickens, to be sure, never began a novel without some sense of where it would go, and particularly in his later novels he drew up fairly detailed plans indicating which characters and events would appear in which installments. This method required, above all, a genius for improvisation. And when we realize just how complex Dickens's plotting tended to be, we can only marvel that he managed to make all the strands come together by the end—and, even more important, made all the plots, subplots, and even sub-subplots cohere. Once these installments appeared, there was of course no opportunity for rethinking or rewriting before the novel itself came out in book form, and therefore many Dickens novels conclude with an obviously hurried attempt to draw things together. The author generally saved this task for the final installment, which was twice as long as its predecessors.

An important advantage of serial publication was the fact that it enabled the novelist to keep his fingers on the pulse of his public. Fluctuations in sales from number to number showed how well the novel was going and which characters were well received. The system afforded the writer an intimacy with his audience that other novelists might well both envy and shun. In a sense, a novel became a cooperative venture between novelist and reader, the latter often deluging the former with

suggestions, pleas, and applause as the plot unfolded. As *The Old Curiosity Shop* was drawing to a close and it gradually became obvious that the heroine was not long for this world, for instance, hundreds of readers urged Dickens not to kill off Little Nell. Dickens resisted their pleas, knowing full well the morbid Victorian relish for the deaths of fictional children, but he did succumb to pressure in giving *Great Expectations* a happier ending than he had intended. His popularity was such that hordes would line up on the Boston docks to await the ship bearing the latest installments of *The Old Curiosity Shop*, eager readers snatching up the latest edition before it could be distributed to local booksellers.

This intimacy with the public was something Dickens's temperament sorely needed; other novelists were less happy with it. As self-conscious an artist as Henry James could never cope with such a

Pickwick Papers was originally conceived of as illustrated satire —with sketches by Robert Seymour and an abbreviated text by a young writer named Charles Dickens. But when Seymour committed suicide early in the project, Dickens had little recourse but to make the drawings (left and right) subservient to the text. The resultant novel made him famous at the tender age of twenty-four.

method of writing, and at the end of the century, when serialization of this sort had largely passed away, George Gissing wrote, in *New Grub Street*, a bitter assault on the demands made on a writer by the three-volume novel, or three-decker, as it was called. Gissing's hero is a novelist of meager imagination but exquisite style who simply cannot produce with the fecundity of a Dickens (whom Gissing greatly admired) and who consequently finds himself forced into sloppy writing and desperate padding to meet his publisher's procrustean demands.

Another ill effect of the combination of serial publication and lending libraries was the prudery it imposed on the novelist. Father would bring home the latest monthly installment of a Dickens novel to read to the family in the evening. When the novel achieved book form, the lending libraries on which most publishers depended for the majority of their sales would not touch it if there was anything in it that, in Victorian parlance, "might bring a blush to the maiden cheek." Thackeray was to complain angrily about this prudery; Dickens somehow lived with it, although it probably had a baleful effect on the conception and treatment of women in his fiction. By the 1890's, under the assaults of Gissing, Hardy, and George Moore, the serial-and-lending-library system had all but disappeared.

On the whole, this was a salutary demise; what we consider the modern novel would have been impossible under it. Yet in the forty-odd years it dominated the English novel it nevertheless produced an astounding number of masterpieces considering its antiaesthetic bias— and, in Charles Dickens, probably the greatest and certainly the best-loved of English novelists.

Dickens's meteoric career bears looking into. The son of a minor clerk in the navy pay office, he spent a happy childhood immersing himself in the fiction of the eighteenth century. But disaster struck in 1824, when Charles was twelve. His father went bankrupt and was sent

to debtors' prison, causing the family to disband almost totally. Charles was sent to work in Warren's Blacking Factory, where his job was to paste labels on pots of shoe blacking. From a happy middle-class childhood he found himself suddenly plunged into the really barbaric depths of the early nineteenth-century proletariat.

Although a fortuitous legacy rescued the family from these straits after Charles had spent only a few months in the blacking factory, he was never to forget the terrible ease with which one could become submerged in society, and much of his subsequent fiction was concerned with the abandonment of a little waif hero or heroine. Certainly Dickens himself determined to make a success of life, and the success he made, beginning at the age of twenty-four, is unparalleled by that of any author at any time.

After a lengthy stint as a court and parliamentary reporter, during which he mastered the then-new technique of shorthand, Dickens began contributing short vignettes of London life to various magazines.

His great opportunity came in 1836 when he was approached to write the letterpress for a series of pictures showing the ludicrous efforts of lower-middle-class types to ape their betters by ineptly indulging in such aristocratic sports as hunting and fishing. When Robert Seymour, the artist around whose pictures Dickens was to weave his text, committed suicide early in the project, Dickens took matters in hand, made the pictures subservient to the text—and produced *Pickwick Papers.*

Here was clearly a vibrant new voice in English fiction. Starting with middling sales, *Pickwick* soon skyrocketed. The high good humor, the fecund creation of character and incident, the brilliant satire of such staid English institutions as parliamentary elections and the Inns of Court took England—and very soon the rest of the world —literally by storm. Ignored were the looseness of construction, the often melodramatic and boring interpolated stories, the sentimentality. Dickens's incomparable humor, combined with a style so vivacious that hardly a dead sentence can be said to exist in any of his massive production, carried the day.

Mere novel writing to formidable deadlines could not satisfy Dickens's immense vitality and his burning need to be loved by as many people as possible. Social criticism, which began in the late chapters of *Pickwick*, set in the Fleet Prison, became an urgent concern, and his lifelong identification with the underdogs of society made him beloved by the common reader. (More aristocratic readers preferred his rival, Thackeray, whose knowledge of high life was indeed more authentic than Dickens's.) A tour of the United States in 1842 confirmed his popularity on the other side of the Atlantic, but Dickens's pleas for American participation in an international copyright agreement met with considerable hostility, for American publishers were regularly pirating his works and not paying a cent in royalties. Moreover, the spectacle of slavery did much to disillusion Dickens, who had held high hopes for American democracy. Still, the tour was not a dead loss, for when the novel he was then working on, *Martin Chuzzlewit*, showed flagging sales, he merely transported most of its major characters to the United States to relive his own adventures there, and sales perked up considerably—vivid testimony to the power for good and ill inherent in serial publication. The American scenes of *Martin Chuzzlewit* remain hilarious and to the point even today, but the serious critic of the novel can only be appalled at the way in which the entire structure is distorted to include the improvised American setting.

To gain further hold on his readers, Dickens also became a magazine editor, spotting such significant new talent as Wilkie Collins and Elizabeth Gaskell, and in 1853 he began a series of public readings from his works that brought him even greater acclaim. Now even the totally illiterate could enjoy Dickens, a born actor, who enthralled his audiences. The emotional energy he poured into his readings was so great that it was a probable cause of his premature death in 1870 at the age of fifty-eight. But no doctors or friends could persuade Dickens to loose this hold on the public, and the readings continued almost unabated until the end of his life, including a totally triumphant tour of the United States in 1867 during which the great novelist came to terms with America, now a member of the international copyright agreement and past its period of slavery.

The nature of Dickens's art is such that none of his fifteen novels stands out as his single masterpiece. Each has glorious and regrettable things in it. The greatness comes from the entire corpus of his work, from the Dickens world that emerges from a reading of all his novels. Often it is a world of outrageous coincidence; of flat, caricatured characters with little existence apart from the tag lines they speak (among them Mrs. Micawber's "I will always be faithful to Mr. Micawber"); of sickening sentimentality, usually associated with his waif children (Little Nell, Paul Dombey, Tiny Tim); of crude melodrama; and of haphazard construction.

Yet on the positive side it is obvious that no other novelist had the powers of imagination, the liveliness of spirit, and the genius of evoking a scene so that even the furniture comes to life that Dickens exercised throughout his career. He is—indeed, he called himself—"The Inimitable," and his popularity, for all its minor fluctuations, has never been greater than it is today, over a century since his death. If many of the functions of his serialized novels have been taken over by television serials, Dickens in the last forty years or so has gained the ever-increasing attention of serious critics, who are finally able to cope with and justify the immense popularity he has always enjoyed among the common readers.

As befits our more troubled times, the later, darker novels of Dickens have won a greater prominence than they enjoyed during the author's lifetime. After the autobiographical *David Copperfield* of 1850, a watershed in mid-career, and under the influence of an unhappy love affair with Ellen Ternan, a young actress whom he met in 1857, Dickens's vision of life changed considerably. The high spirits and improvisation of such earlier novels as *Nicholas Nickleby* and *Martin Chuzzlewit* gave way to a more somber view of life and more conscious artistic control. Serial installments did not necessarily have to end in a cliff-hanging denouement; pure humor is either muted or becomes bitter satire; easy melodrama becomes genuine tragedy; and conscious symbolic structure governs the action of such later masterpieces as *Bleak House*, *Great Expectations*, and *Our Mutual Friend*. The Victorian stick-figure heroine, usually the dullest and least convincing character in an early Dickens novel, takes on the dark allure of Ellen Ternan in the later ones, and for the first time Dickens is prepared to cope with sexual obsession and jealousy. Meanwhile, his fury at the outrageous injustices of society becomes increasingly despairing until, in *Hard Times*, no segment of society escapes his wrath save for an itinerant band of circus performers who bring the only spot of joy to England's industralized Midlands.

This is the Dickens who has exercised the most influence on our times, when he has come to be seen as the greatest of the Victorian prophets, far outranking the once-mighty Carlyle and Ruskin. This is not the humorous-sentimental Dickens of whom Thackeray once declared, flinging down in despair the latest serial installment of *Dombey and Son*: "There's no writing against such power as this—one

Neither friends nor doctors could persuade Dickens to curtail the public readings that were so detrimental to his health. His triumphal tour of America in 1867-68 (above) was so emotionally and physically fatiguing that he collapsed upon his return to England. Never fully recovering, Dickens died in 1870 and lies buried with national honors in Westminster Abbey.

has no chance!" It was that Dickens whom Thackeray came to rival in the 1850's—looming larger than it is possible to imagine today. Snobs who deprecated Dickens either on aesthetic or social grounds—for the slipshod nature of his plotting or his unfamiliarity with upper-class types—saw his superior in Thackeray; and, indeed, in his masterpiece, *Vanity Fair*, Thackeray achieved a kind of perfection within the scope of Victorian conventions not to be found in any single novel of Dickens's. With Dickens the entire oeuvre is what counts; with Thackeray almost everything except *Vanity Fair* has been forgotten.

Born in India in 1811, seven months before Dickens, Thackeray was sent to school in England when, shortly after the death of his father, his mother remarried. Presumably this was the equivalent trauma in his development to the blacking factory episode in Dickens's youth. Lanky, myopic, and terribly shy, Thackeray found himself plunged into the snobbish, rough-and-tumble schoolboy world of the Charterhouse School. He then spent an unhappy year at Cambridge before traveling about Europe studying law and painting in a desultory way. It was as a would-be artist, in fact, that his path first crossed Dickens's. On the death of Robert Seymour, Thackeray was one of the artists Dickens had interviewed to complete the illustrations for *Pickwick Papers*. Dickens didn't care for Thackeray's pictures, however, and the personal coolness between the two men may have stemmed from that early encounter.

Thackeray then began contributing articles to a variety of popular magazines of the day, most notably to the newly founded *Punch*. The series of satiric sketches later published as *The Book of Snobs* that he wrote for *Punch* in 1846–47 mark the emergence of a great novelist, for in his anatomization of snobs—and, in a later series, *Mr. Punch's Prize Novelists*, of various kinds of bad novels—Thackeray was able to channel his immense satiric gifts into a full-blown novel for the first time. *Vanity Fair* began appearing in monthly serial numbers in 1847, the year of *Jane Eyre* and *Wuthering Heights*, but it is as unlike those novels as it is possible to be.

For the private world of intensely felt grand passion that the Brontës exposed, Thackeray substituted a vast comic panorama of English social life at about the time of the Napoleonic Wars. If his characters tended to be caricatures, this fault was made a virtue both by Thackeray's sophisticated awareness of it—he keeps referring to them as puppets—and by his unfailing satiric wit, which doesn't require characterization in depth to make its points. Above all, Thackeray was able to give his sprawling novel a tight structure such as the early Dickens was incapable of. By pitting two heroines against each other, and by following the upward social climb of Becky Sharp as it crosses the downward path of Amelia, he gave the novel a firmer skeleton than one could expect in a vast social novel of the time—let alone a serialized one. And by subtitling it "A Novel Without a Hero," he was clearly challenging conventional attitudes to heroism, to the relations of the sexes (Becky is really a female Napoleon), and to the military versus the civilian virtues. In a way, *Vanity Fair* is rather like an English *War and Peace*—without the war.

William Makepeace Thackeray studied painting in Paris for three years before forsaking art for authorship. In addition to the self-portrait above, he illustrated many of his own satiric sketches of upper- and middle-class English life. Samples from Our Street *appear at right.*

Although he wrote a half-dozen or so novels in addition to *Vanity Fair*, the only other one to survive to our day has been *Henry Esmond*, a historical novel about the early eighteenth century that is infinitely more sophisticated than any of Scott's works—a triumph of pastiche in which Thackeray, who loved the eighteenth century and understood its style to perfection, was able to imitate the High Augustan style of Addison and Swift so successfully that it is hard to believe the novel was written by a Victorian. Yet the same urbane disillusionment of *Vanity Fair* pervades *Henry Esmond*; it lacks perhaps only the wit of the earlier novel to make it an equal triumph.

If Thackeray was not as great an artist as his contemporaries thought, he was far too great a novelist to deserve his current neglect, which is based partly on his cloying sentimentality, partly on his habit of introducing personal comments into his narratives in a way deemed inartistic by recent generations. Read properly, with no dogmatic assumptions about what should constitute the metaphysics of the novel, Thackeray looms very large indeed.

With the death of Thackeray in 1863 and of Dickens seven years later, the Victorian novel entered a new phase, one signaled by the rise of George Eliot and Thomas Hardy. Virginia Woolf once said of George Eliot's masterpiece, *Middlemarch*, that it was "one of the few English novels written for adult people." Understood correctly, this comment fits not only the work of Eliot and Hardy, but illuminates the difference between late and early Victorian fiction.

One of the peculiarities of the English novel is that almost from its birth it has furnished works readable both by adults and children. The concept of a special literature designed for the young is a relatively recent one, dating back only to the late eighteenth century. Previously, and for many years afterward, children were considered to be little adults, in dress, behavior, and reading habits as well. Thus we find Dickens, for instance, claiming to have read in his childhood the novels of Defoe, Fielding, and Smollett—books certainly not written for children. "I have been Tom Jones (a child's Tom Jones, a harmless creature) for a week together," he once wrote. "I have sustained my own idea of Roderick Random for a month at a stretch, I verily believe." With no body of children's literature to draw on, the adult fiction of the eighteenth century seems to have served Dickens just as well, and he in turn wrote novels perhaps best encountered first in childhood or early adolescence.

The popularity of Dickens and many other English novelists among children (at least at a time when children read at all) can throw an unnecessary roadblock in the way of adults who fail to realize that the appeal of much English fiction to children does not preclude an even deeper appeal to grownups. *Wuthering Heights*, for instance, is a titanic, complex masterpiece notwithstanding the fact that it also sweeps adolescent girls off their feet. The English novel somehow manages to run on both juvenile and adult tracks at once, seldom getting derailed by either puerility or esotericism.

Yet with *Middlemarch* we are clearly in a new genre that exerts its fascination only on a totally adult mind. "Of all English novelists," one critic has written, "George Eliot has the best mind"—which is not to say she is the best novelist, but that she is something very different from those we have encountered before: a conscious intellectual writing only for thinking people. This seems strange when one considers how many schoolchildren have been afflicted with her earlier novel, *Silas Marner*, and it is very difficult to expunge from the adult mind horrible memories of that premature encounter. *Silas Marner* remains minor Eliot, but read in maturity, *Middlemarch* can have a staggering effect sufficient to make one appreciate the justice of the many critics who claim it is the greatest of all English novels.

George Eliot was the pen name of Mary Ann Evans, born in 1819, the daughter of an estate agent for a wealthy Warwickshire family. A serious, religious girl, she slowly and painfully shed her provincial evangelicalism and educated herself to the extent that she was able to translate, when she was just twenty-six, a hefty German scholarly tome entitled *The Life of Jesus*, and to contribute articles to the prestigious *Westminster Review*.

In 1851 she met George Henry Lewes, himself an awesome scholar and Goethe authority, and from 1854 until his death in 1878 they lived as man and wife, although they never married. Ordinarily such a ménage would have shocked Victorian England, but such were the obvious high intellectual and moral qualities of the union that all its irregularity did was spare the couple the attentions of time-wasting fools and prudes and let them live and work together within a small,

Mary Ann Evans, whose pen name was George Eliot, was almost forty before she wrote her first fiction. Perhaps because of this she brought a new degree of maturity and insight to the Victorian novel. Her works are a realistic observation of the world of peasants and townspeople, but this realism is deepened by a profound concern for the grave moral problems of her time.

Overleaf: The Travelling Companions, *by Augustus Leopold Egg, suggests something of the vogue the Victorian novel enjoyed among the leisure classes.*

protective, and tight-knit circle of understanding friends.

It was Lewes who first inspired Mary Ann Evans to write novels under the pen name of George Eliot; her first fiction was *Scenes of Clerical Life*, a collection of three long stories that was published in 1858 when she was nearly forty. Thus, from the beginning of her career she brought to novel writing a maturity, both chronological and intellectual, that allowed for no false starts, no faults of amateurishness or of inexperience.

Scenes of Clerical Life was followed by *Adam Bede*, her first great success, and that by *The Mill on the Floss* and *Silas Marner*. Without enjoying quite the epidemic popularity of Dickens, George Eliot was building a solid and respectable reputation as a novelist, and her early books are still her most loved. They dwell much on the English countryside of her girlhood and deal with moral dilemmas minutely and sympathetically analyzed from a standpoint that is puritanical but never dogmatic or merely pious. In these early novels a fine mind and a feeling heart were merging, and with *Middlemarch* in 1872, George Eliot brought all her gifts to perfection.

One of the unique features of *Middlemarch* as the supremely adult Victorian novel is that it deals with the condition of marriage, something most Victorian novelists either ignored or took for granted. The characteristic Dickens novel ends with hero and heroine finally wed after a most hectic courtship, presumably to live eternally in nuptial bliss, surrounded by many rosy-cheeked children. Dickens, whose own marriage, though fecund, was unhappy, did not particularly respond as an artist to the institution. George Eliot, who did not marry until 1880, the year of her death, applies the finest analytical eye in all English fiction to the marriages in *Middlemarch*, and perhaps it might be said that not only could no child fully appreciate the novel, but neither could anyone who has not been married.

But *Middlemarch* is about more than marriage. It is about the drag toward mediocrity exerted on idealists and men and women of good will by provincial society and the dead hand of the past. Over its long course we see the gradual diminution of ideals of its finest people, Dorothea Brooke and Tertius Lydgate; a diminution brought about not merely by the humdrum town of Middlemarch in which they live but also—and this is the finest of Eliot's perceptions—by flaws in their own characters, by what she calls the "spots of commonness" that prevent us from becoming the great men and women we dream of being. The rampant egoism of even the most seemingly self-abnegating among us militates against our success in life, whether it be in marriage, medicine, or philanthropy, and the subtlety of Eliot's psychological, social, and moral analysis of the effects of egoism—in addition to her mastery in dramatizing these effects in realistic form—make for the great impact of her novel.

Both in her life and her art, George Eliot challenged many a shibboleth of Victorian society, but throughout her work there is an almost Shakespearian acceptance of reality as it exists. Thomas Hardy, on the other hand, threw down the gauntlet to the Victorian world of home, hearth, and child labor with such passion and tragic outrage that it

never quite recovered. He both ended the Victorian novel and began the modern novel, and like George Eliot he, too, can really be appreciated only by adult readers.

When Hardy was born in 1840, England was only semi-industrialized; the railroad was a relatively new mode of transportation and the Napoleonic Wars were still a lively memory in the minds of many. When he died in 1928, air travel was becoming a commonplace and England had experienced a world war. Thus his extraordinarily long life spanned an almost complete transformation of the peaceful, rural society into which he was born into a world very like the present one.

Keenly aware of these changes, Hardy sought out the eternal verities in his native Dorset, in southernmost England, which he transformed into the imaginary county of Wessex, where life proceeded at its immemorial pace. Like George Eliot, he was deeply rooted in the English soil, and like her he found much comedy and wisdom in the speech and folkways of yeomen and farmers. But unlike her, and unlike almost all other Victorians, he also saw that there was something terribly wrong in the eternal scheme of things. He was not concerned with attacking such specific abuses as the Poor Laws, as Dickens had done in *Oliver Twist*, or snobbery, as Thackeray had done in *Vanity Fair*. Hardy's fiction is concerned with more basic injustices in the cosmos; it is nothing less than a savage attack on the indifference of the gods to men, on the "crass casualty" of events, as he expressed it in an early poem. He, then, is at least as much Greek in spirit as English.

Hardy set out to be an architect—ironically, considering his later agnosticism—specializing in church restoration, a major Victorian architectural concern. His early faith dissipated under the influences of Charles Darwin, Herbert Spencer, and Thomas Huxley, whom he avidly read as a young man, and he found himself tearing down with his literary art the underlying assumptions of those very churches he was rebuilding with his architectural art. By the time he was thirty, Hardy had more or less completely abandoned architecture for literature.

He began his second career as a poet, turning to fiction and laboriously mastering the techniques of the popular Victorian novel only when it became apparent he could not earn a living as a poet. Yet many modern critics consider Hardy an even greater poet than he is a novelist, and when his last novel, *Jude the Obscure*, aroused a storm of protest from clergy and critics alike, Hardy returned to his first love, writing nothing but poetry for the last thirty years of his life.

Both architecture and poetry exercised a profound influence on his fictional art. He tended to build his novels like great Gothic cathedrals, block set upon block of related incidents with a symmetry, a massiveness, and a solidity of form rare among Victorian novelists. Occasionally his architectural concern for symmetry led him to force characters into unbelievable postures and to manipulate plot into a dependence on tortuous coincidences, but read sympathetically, Hardy's novels do have a grandeur of form, a heroic effort to impose form on chaotic human activities within a meaningless universe, that is very moving.

The poet in Hardy contributed to a poetry of concept, situation, and mood, yet like many great poets Hardy was often an indifferent

The works of Thomas Hardy (left) are imbued with the English soil. His native Dorset (below) was to become "Wessex" in novels that are both traditional and modern at the same time. For while his works are a celebration of the eternal verities of country life, nineteenth-century determinism is displayed in characters who struggle but are ultimately defeated by their social and physical environment.

writer of prose. The rugged Anglo-Saxon diction, the craggy, hyper-Browningesque verse lines that distinguish Hardy's poetry often make for mere awkwardness in his prose, which can be horribly stilted and flat. Like Theodore Dreiser, Hardy was a great novelist but often an embarrassingly amateurish writer. Of his eighteen novels and collections of short stories, five seem destined to endure: *Far From the Madding Crowd, The Return of the Native, The Mayor of Casterbridge, Tess of the D'Urbervilles*, and *Jude the Obscure*. As time went on, Hardy increasingly turned away from merely chronicling what Gray called "the short and simple annals of the poor," launching a bitter assault on the world around him. Critical outrage at what was considered Hardy's outspoken sexuality but what really must have been his profound pessimism increased as his career progressed, turning him finally back to poetry, in which he could say the same things to a smaller, more sympathetic audience.

In his final masterpiece, *Jude the Obscure*, Hardy offers his most powerful indictment of things as they are. His hero is a stonemason (as Hardy's father and grandfather had been) who yearns for an education leading to the ministry at Christminster, an amalgam of Oxford and Cambridge. But Christminster will not accept so humbly born a student, and Jude is seduced into a disastrous marriage with an earthy farm girl and an even more disastrous liaison with Sue Bridehead, Hardy's vision of the neurotic, frigid "new woman" of the 1890's, a terrible sister of Ibsen's Nora. Torn between his sensual needs and his spiritual aspirations, Jude dies in Joblike despair.

Although the novel contains many outright attacks on the marriage and divorce laws of the time, as well as discriminatory university admission policies, the greatness of *Jude the Obscure* is not diminished one whit by the fact that those laws and policies have all been liberalized. Hardy is not a reformer like Dickens or Zola; at his best he digs so deep into the tragic nature of existence that no amount of mere political or social reform can ameliorate the torment of his characters. Hardy's real quarrel is with God, not society. Technically flawed and often ill-written as his novels are, they remain the most powerful Victorian statement we have of man's unhappy lot in the cosmos: Hardy ranges from potboiling Victorian hack at his worst to Aeschylean tragic seer at his best, and there are times when both aspects of him coexist in the same novel.

By the time Hardy had ended his career as a novelist, in 1895, an entirely different reading public had come into existence from the one that had largely ignored Jane Austen at the beginning of the century. Nearly universal primary education, ever-increasing literacy, cheaper methods of publication, more rapid means of communication—all had taken the reading of novels out of the hands of the few and put it in the hands of many. The vast popularity of Dickens, the moral intensity of Eliot, the philosophical questioning of Hardy had shown once and for all that "mere novels" were not necessarily confined to a readership of idle young ladies and their mammas hoping to while away a lazy hour or two in the sanctity of their boudoirs. What Henry James called "the great form" had arrived.

3

Romance, Realism, Remembrance

ACROSS THE ENGLISH CHANNEL in France, literary developments closely paralleled those occurring in Great Britain. Although one scholar has estimated that some 1,250 "novels" were published in France during the seventeenth century, these tended to be either lengthy, unrealistic romances or crudely extravagant burlesques rather than what we would consider novels. François Rabelais's five-volume masterpiece, *Gargantua and Pantagruel*, has meant many things to many readers since the first part of it was published in 1532, but to call it a novel would be stretching even that protean form beyond any meaningful limits. Like *Gulliver's Travels*, which it influenced, *Gargantua and Pantagruel* is *sui generis*.

By the eighteenth century, however, Alain-René Lesage was writing picaresque novels—of which *Gil Blas de Santillane* is the most famous —that were to influence Smollett deeply. The Anglophile Abbé Prévost most admired Richardson and ultimately translated his novels into French; his *Histoire du Chevalier des Grieux et Manon Lescaut* anticipates *Pamela*—at least in its fluttering feminine "sensibility"—by a decade. And Jean-Jacques Rousseau adapted both the sensibility and the epistolary technique of Richardson for his *La Nouvelle Héloïse*, published two decades after *Pamela*. The sole novel of Choderlos de Laclos, *Les Liaisons dangereuses*, was also written in the form of letters, but Laclos, a general in Napoleon's army, substituted a harshly cynical view of the relations between the sexes for Richardson's sentimental-moralistic one. In the nineteenth century, the influence of Scott, first translated into French in 1822, was felt in such historical novels as Alfred de Vigny's *Cinq-Mars*, Honoré de Balzac's *Les Chouans*, and Victor Hugo's *Notre-Dame de Paris*. The historical romances of Alexandre Dumas *père* (*The Count of Monte Cristo; The Three Musketeers*) achieved a popularity analagous to that of Dickens by similar methods of serialization.

The bookstalls that line the banks of the Seine are as much a fixture of Paris today as they were in 1843, when William Parrott painted the scene at left.

It would be a mistake, however, to emphasize Anglo-French influences too strongly, for in most important ways the French handling of fiction is unique. For one thing, the French have always excelled—as the English have not—at the short novel, or novella. Some of the greatest French novels are briefer than anything comparable in England. Such works as Diderot's *Rameau's Nephew*, Voltaire's *Candide*, Chateaubriand's *Atala*, Mérimée's *Carmen*, Flaubert's *Three Stories*, and

51

Colette's *The Cat* are uniquely French in the power they manage to exert in brief form. Longer than short stories but shorter than standard novels, these masterpieces—and many more like them—have no parallel in English fiction. Significantly, the French have also produced some of the best long novels in the world, from Madeleine de Scudéry's *Artamène, ou le Grand Cyrus* in the seventeenth century through Hugo's *Les Misérables* in the nineteenth to Proust's *Remembrance of Things Past* in the twentieth. But the very capacity of the French mind and language for concise, pithy expression has made the French among the most illustrious practitioners of the novella, while the English genius seems to require breadth and amplitude to express itself properly.

Another unique strength of the French novel is its capacity for intensive moral and psychological analysis. This begins with what most people would recognize as the first truly great French novel, Comtesse de La Fayette's *The Princess of Clèves* (1678), and reaches such stag-

LA
PRINCESSE
DE
CLEVES.
TOME I.

PARIS,
Chez CLAVDE BARBIN, au Palais,
fur le fecond Perron de la Sainte
Chapelle.

M. DC. LXXVIII.
AVEC PRIVILEGE DV ROY.

Rabelais's five-volume satiric masterpiece, Gargantua and Pantagruel, *from which the engraving at left is taken, was first published in the mid-sixteenth century. It strongly influenced both Voltaire and Swift, but it cannot fairly be called the first French novel. That honor belongs to* The Princess of Clèves *(above), whose author, Mme de La Fayette (top, right), set a precedent for intense moral and psychological analysis that became a key characteristic of the French novel. Her literary heirs include Choderlos de Laclos, whose* Les Liaisons dangereuses *is illustrated at near right, and Victor Hugo (far right), France's champion of romanticism.*

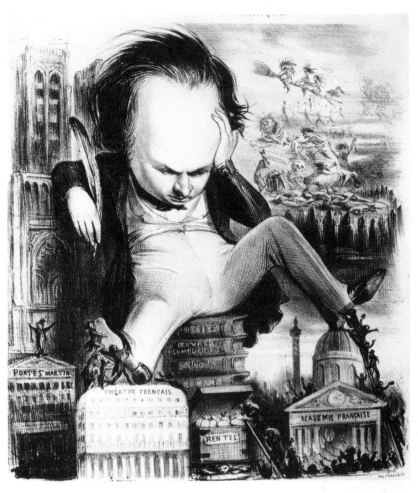

gering culmination in Proust's *Remembrance of Things Past* (1913-27) that it is difficult to imagine the novel of introspective analysis going any further. Indeed, since Proust's death the French novel has taken a very different turn, for like many of the supreme artists of the world Proust was the end rather than the beginning of a tradition.

Mme de La Fayette was connected by friendship to the court of Louis XIV at Versailles, and like those great court gossips Saint-Simon and Mme de Sévigné she developed a sharp eye for the elaborate social intercourse of the period. She was also an intimate friend of the duc de la Rochefoucauld, whose *Maxims* remain unchallenged to this day for their cynical moral insights expressed with incomparable terse wit. Nevertheless, *The Princess of Clèves* is a sober, austere handling of that favorite theme of such contemporary dramatists as Corneille and Racine, the clash between passionate love and social duty.

Mme de La Fayette ultimately comes down on the side of duty, but she is keenly aware that to do one's duty is not always the happiest of alternatives. Her mantle of psychological and moral introspection eventually passed on to Choderlos de Laclos, whose masterpiece of a century later, *Les Liaisons dangereuses*, seems moralistic only as an after-

It was while stationed in Civita-vecchia as consul that Henri Beyle (left) embarked on his extraordinary novelistic career. Under the pen name Stendhal he produced one of his greatest novels, The Charterhouse of Parma. A rendering of the Parmesan monastery of the title appears below. Stendhal's literary opposite was Honoré de Balzac (right). Where the former's prose was spare and dry, the latter wrote like a man possessed, and then rewrote entire books in galley proof (above).

thought. For the bulk of the novel its vicious protagonists, Valmont and Mme de Merteuil, seduce and debauch their innocent victims with no apparent comment or intervention by the author. Valmont in particular is reminiscent of the rake Lovelace in *Clarissa*, but Laclos's moral neutrality and inbuilt cynicism are leagues apart from Richardson. In many ways complementary works, *Clarissa* and *Les Liaisons dangereuses* taken together form the absolute pinnacle of the epistolary novel, and are therefore a dead end for that genre.

In 1783, the year after *Les Liaisons dangereuses* was published, Laclos's heir—and literary superior—was born. Henri Beyle, like Laclos, served in Napoleon's army in the equivalent of the quartermaster's corps, and he picked up the pen name by which he would become famous, Stendhal, from a small German town the army passed through. (Beyle, a complex man of many masks, loved pen names; some of his others were Mr. Myself, Old Hummums, and William Crocodile.) Stendhal accompanied Napoleon on the disastrous Russian campaign of

54

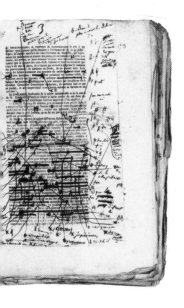

1812, but after Waterloo he found himself, like so many ambitious young men who had hitched their wagons to Napoleon's fallen star, out of work and ill at ease in a world where business chicanery had supplanted military valor. For a time he lived a dilettante's life in Paris and Milan, scratching up a living by undertaking such hack-work projects as travel books, biographies of Haydn and Rossini, and that almost obligatory book for a Frenchman, a treatise on love, about which Stendhal was an outstanding authority if only a spotty practitioner. Many passages of these early works were simply plagiarized; a far smaller number show glints of the great novelist to come. In 1831 he was made consul in the small, unimportant Italian town of Civitavecchia, where he remained five years, neglecting his duties while working on his extraordinary novels and memoirs.

Stendhal's two greatest novels are *The Red and the Black* (1830), which is based, like Dreiser's *An American Tragedy*, on an actual murder case, and *The Charterhouse of Parma* (1839), which André

Souvenir de Balzac à Villedavray - 1840

Gide, like many before and after him, considered the greatest of all French novels. In both, as well as in the uncompleted *Lucien Leuwen*, Stendhal treated the predicament of ambitious youth in post-Napoleonic France and Italy with unfailing wit and psychological insight, in a style so spare and dry—in the way that champagne is dry—and so effective that Stendhal himself admitted it was derived from the Code Napoléon, the French legal code. Combining the best of the classical and romantic temperaments, Stendhal was so far ahead of his time in his total lack of sentimentality that he dedicated his works "To the Happy Few" and predicted they would only begin to be appreciated by about 1880 and would only fully come into their own in the 1920's. As usual, he was right.

One of the "happy few" was Honoré de Balzac, whose long, effusive review of *The Charterhouse of Parma* appeared shortly before Stendhal's death in 1842. Balzac's own prodigious genius was poles apart from Stendhal's, for where the latter was ironic, skeptical, and witty, the former was romantic, often mystical, and entirely megalomaniacal. "What Napoleon achieved by the sword I shall achieve by the pen," he once vowed, and he set about doing so in the seventy-odd volumes of his *La Comédie humaine*, a vast panorama of loosely interrelated novels dealing with nothing less than the whole of French life in the early nineteenth century and featuring a cast of some two thousand characters.

Divided into such categories as "Scenes of Private Life," "Scenes of Provincial Life," and "Scenes of Parisian Life," *La Comédie humaine* first appeared between 1842 and 1848. Perhaps the work's most impres-

The immense factual detail with which Balzac filled his novels makes him one of the first French realists. His masterpiece, La Comédie humaine, is an ambitious attempt to portray every aspect of human life in early-nineteenth-century France. This enormous body of interrelated novels is divided into three groups and further subdivided into five categories. Balzac's research for one of the categories, "Scenes of Provincial Life," included the foray to Avray depicted above. The Panthéon, seen in a period engraving opposite, was described in equal detail in Le Père Goriot.

AUX GRANDS HOMMES LA PATRIE RECONNAISSANTE

sive feature is its sheer fecundity. Dressed in a monk's robe and quaffing innumerable cups of strong black coffee, Balzac wrote throughout the night, churning out novel after novel. He then desperately rewrote entire novels in galley proof, a hectic and expensive procedure that completely wore him out by the age of fifty-one. Somehow he also found the time to set himself up as a somewhat ludicrous dandy who bought gloves and bejeweled walking sticks by the dozen; to woo and win a variety of aristocratic women despite his ever-increasing corpulence; and to lose most of the money he had made from writing by backing several business ventures as ill-fated as the ones Mark Twain would invest in later in the century.

Given Balzac's demonic drive, it is hardly startling that his novels are variable in quality; the startling fact is how great so many of them are. Although he often wrote carelessly, practically every page of Balzac seems imbued with his own immense vitality, and such novels as *Le Père Goriot*, *Eugénie Grandet*, and *Lost Illusions* are not merely isolated masterpieces, but, taken with the whole of *La Comédie humaine*, offer an unparalleled picture of an entire society set forth in unremitting, fascinating detail.

With his comprehensive, almost obsessive command of detail, Balzac could be considered at least as much a realist as a romantic, which is also true of his great successor, Gustave Flaubert, although the fastidious Flaubert despised any such literary catchwords and brought to the realistic nineteenth-century French novel a single-minded obsession

Gustave Flaubert (right) was even more obsessed with detail than was Balzac. His novels were scrupulously researched, and he spent days hunting for "le mot juste"—the exactly right word to express a particular nuance of meaning and feeling. In his most famous novel, Madame Bovary, *the strictures of bourgeois society in Rouen (left, below) are juxtaposed against the romantic yearnings of the novel's heroine, Emma Bovary (left, above).*

with pure artistry uncharacteristic of the prodigious Balzac. Both men were driven megalomaniacs, but in different ways. Balzac had to write more novels, encompassing more of society, than anyone else. Flaubert was contented with writing very few novels, but would spend days and weeks mulling over problems of structure and style in his dedicated search for what he called *"le mot juste"*—the perfect, the only, word to express his thought. Balzac's genius was the triumph of vitality over slovenliness; Flaubert's the triumph of perfection of style over the often seedy and unworthy materials that nineteenth-century French bourgeois life presented to him.

Like Balzac before him and Proust after, Flaubert essentially lived the life of a hermit, sequestering himself on his mother's estate in pure dedication to his art. His work took two forms: the realistic novel of contemporary life (*Madame Bovary* and *The Sentimental Education*), and highly colored, romantic novels of the distant past (*The Temptation of St. Anthony* and *Salammbô*). The only common denominator

between these seemingly disparate genres is the immense amount of detailed research that went into them. Whether he did his research in libraries to evoke brilliantly the life of ancient Carthage, as in *Salammbô*, or simply used the keenness of his observation of contemporary mores, as in *Madame Bovary*, Flaubert took infinite pains with his material even before setting pen to paper. Then would come the struggle for *"le mot juste"* so that the expression would do justice to the perceptions. Flaubert was the most self-conscious artist of all novelists up to his time.

The first appearance of *Madame Bovary* in the *Revue de Paris* in 1856 aroused such indignation on the part of the bourgeoisie it so remorselessly flayed that Flaubert was prosecuted for offending public morals. After a sensational trial—at the same time that Baudelaire was being tried on similar charges for his volume of poems, *Les Fleurs du mal*—the novelist was acquitted. It is still easy to see why *Madame Bovary* should raise middle-class hackles the way it did. Pitting a foolishly romantic, adulterous heroine against stupid, smug, bourgeois provincial society, and treating the ensuing conflict with relentless objectivity and barely latent scorn, Flaubert achieved a triumph of art. Yet even so admiring a critic as Henry James felt that its author had expended more art on *Madame Bovary* than the subject warranted; and there was a discrepancy between Flaubert's essentially sordid and barren material and the elegance of his treatment. Contemporary readers, however, saw it only as an attack on the brutish complacency of their lives, and they resented it accordingly.

Flaubert's single-minded dedication to the art of fiction drew around him a whole circle of friends and admirers, among them the great Russian novelist Ivan Turgenev and the most brilliant of disciples, Guy de Maupassant, whose family knew Flaubert's. Although Maupassant wrote six novels, he is best remembered for his sixteen volumes of short stories. Like Flaubert, he drew his materials from life in his native Normandy and treated it with irony, clarity, and realism. Yet Maupassant was a less fastidious artist than his mentor, and often produced work of journalistic rather than purely literary quality. The surprise endings of such tales as "The Necklace" have not worn too well, partly because the technique was later vulgarized by O. Henry and innumerable minor magazine hacks. Yet in such stories of the Franco-Prussian War of 1870 as "Ball of Fat" and "Mademoiselle Fifi," Maupassant achieved Flaubertian heights of artistry. They have become such classics that "Ball of Fat," transformed to the American West, still showed considerable power as the basis for John Ford's movie *Stagecoach*.

Maupassant shared Flaubert's contempt for the middle class. A vigorous sportsman, he would often spend his Sundays rowing half-nude up the Seine, shouting imprecations at the startled country folk as they filed complacently out of church for their Sunday dinners. Maupassant's robust appearance was deceptive, however, for he died mad at forty-two, a victim of syphilis and overwork, before his splendid talents could reach full fruition.

The last major French novelistic talent of the nineteenth century was Emile Zola, who in many ways resembles a less imaginative Balzac.

By the late nineteenth century, the realism of Balzac and Flaubert had evolved into naturalism. The distinction between the two schools is a fine one, but naturalism brought to the novel an objectivity and detachment previously reserved for the subject matter of science. Emile Zola (left, in a famous portrait by Edouard Manet), was a leading exponent of naturalism who applied scientific precision in the service of social reform.

Overleaf: Les Halles, the great produce market known as "The Stomach of Paris," was the object of Zola's clinical eye in a novel called Le Ventre de Paris.

Like Balzac, Zola was, for all his surface prosaicness, a great poet of ordinary life in Paris, which he rendered with verve and documentary accuracy. He was also like Balzac, Thackeray, and so many lesser nineteenth-century novelists in that he saw the ways in which fortunes were made and unmade in the increasingly fluid society of the nineteenth century. Hitherto, a man's rank in life had been largely determined by his ancestry. But with the French Revolution, the Industrial Revolution, and the ever-burgeoning capitalism that came in its wake, it became possible for the first time to rise from the lowest to the highest rungs of society, and conversely to fall, to become *déclassé*, through one misstep—an unfortunate marriage, say, or a lack of will to compete with social inferiors. Stendhal's heroes, while ambitious, are too proud and self-aware to pummel their way to the pig trough of

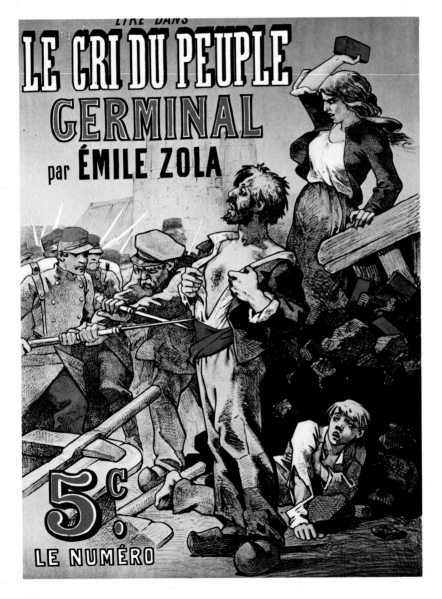

mercantile success. Balzac, far more vulgar and himself a self-made man, exulted in the quest for fame and money as much as his hero Rastignac, who once stood on the heights of Père-Lachaise Cemetery overlooking all of Paris and vowed: "It's war between us now!" Zola's figures, on the other hand, tend to be defeated by a materialistic determinism beyond their scope of comprehension. But in the great tradition of the nineteenth-century novel, he nevertheless seems to be showing us society as a giant bank of escalators, with some characters inexorably rising while others descend.

Like Balzac, Zola too thought in grandiose terms; his equivalent of *La Comédie humaine* is the twenty Rougon-Macquart novels that

Social injustice was to motivate much of Zola's art. Germinal (opposite) was an 1885 exposé of the bitter suffering of French miners. A decade later Zola was to become equally involved in the plight of Alfred Dreyfus (right and below), the Jewish officer who was convicted of treason and drummed out of the French army. When it became apparent Dreyfus had been framed, Zola penned J'accuse *(above).*

Overleaf: Proust was as committed a Dreyfusard as Zola, but there the similarity between the two writers ends. Proust's Paris was restricted to the gardens and salons of the upper class.

appeared between 1871 and 1893. This series attempts to trace the inheritance of characteristics within one family, thus furnishing what Zola himself was to call "the natural and social history of a family in the Second Empire."

Zola set about his self-imposed task with at least as much of a scientist's attitude as that of a novelist. By about 1865, under the influence of the historian-critic Hippolyte Taine and the physiological experiments of Dr. Claude Bernard, the realism of Balzac and Flaubert had become what is known as naturalism. The distinction is a delicate one. Essentially, naturalism entails the application of documentary, quasi-scientific realism to the lower strata of society, while realism is much broader both in social and aesthetic range. This Zola did with compulsive zeal. Notebook in hand, he went to live among miners, jotting down everything he saw, heard or smelled in order to produce his novel of mining life, *Germinal*. The food-market district of Paris, Les Halles, underwent similar scrutiny to produce *Le Ventre de Paris;* department

stores to furnish the material for *Au Bonheur des Dames*; alcoholics for *L'Assommoir*, and so forth. What Zola's research methods were for *Nana*, his great study of the lives and morals of Second Empire courtesans, it is difficult to say, but through all his novels the note of authenticity of documentation rings loud and clear.

Unfortunately, the naturalists in general and Zola in particular tended to let research take the place of imagination, so that what we often get in their novels is a kind of photographic representation of life rather than the deeply conceived oil paintings of a Balzac. Furthermore, as his career progressed, Zola became increasingly attracted to the socialist cause, introducing an element of propagandizing into his fiction that tended further to vitiate his art.

It was his moral conscience, however, that led to what may have been Zola's finest hour. In 1892 he had published *La Débâcle*, a fiercely honest account of the causes of France's ignominious defeat in the Franco-Prussian War, a conflict that most Frenchmen would have preferred to forget. Like many of Zola's novels, *La Débâcle* aroused cries of outrage from the chauvinists of the right. This was nothing, however, compared to the explosion of the Dreyfus affair two years later, in which Alfred Dreyfus, a Jewish officer of impeccable patriotic credentials, was falsely accused of having passed important military secrets to the German embassy.

Dreyfus's subsequent trial, conviction, and imprisonment on Devil's Island proved a national disgrace even more searing than the Franco-Prussian War. It polarized France between the generally liberal Dreyfusards and the aristocratic, clerical, military, anti-Semitic right wing of French society that had nurtured its grievances ever since the French Revolution. Even the totally apolitical Proust was to get involved, col-

The genius of Proust (far left) looms as large in the history of the French novel as does the genius of Joyce in the English-speaking world. Colette (left) was to inherit the former's sensuality but little of his analytical genius. André Gide (above), on the other hand, carried precision of analysis too far; in his works, the cerebral completely over-whelms the visceral. Gide's antithesis can be found in the nose-thumbing surrealism of Jean Cocteau (far right).

lecting signatures on behalf of Dreyfus from his friends in high society. But of all French novelists, Zola's role in the affair was the most spectacular. As evidence began to mount that Dreyfus had been framed by one Major Esterhazy, Zola published the famous *J'accuse*, an open letter to the president of the French Republic that accused the war office of grave injustices and insisted on a reopening of the case. Ultimately Dreyfus was acquitted, reinstated in the army, and served with distinction in World War I. But at the time of the affair, Zola was pilloried in the right-wing press and later sentenced to a year in prison for libel. He escaped to England for a year, returning to France in 1902 only to die bizarrely of accidental carbon monoxide poisoning from a faulty stove.

Zola was in so many ways an admirable man and a powerful polemicist and novelist that it seems a pity he was not more of an artist. Yet while the Rougon-Macquart series remains an impressive achievement, and while individual novels in it have lost little of their strength over the years, that strength is increasingly seen as essentially journalistic rather than novelistic. In a sense Zola was the captive of a theory of fiction that suited his talents all too well but that has increasingly shown its limitations as a valid principle upon which great fiction can be constructed.

Such is not the case with Zola's fellow defender of Dreyfus, Marcel Proust, who looms ever larger not only as France's greatest novelist but possibly as the greatest novelist of all time. This posthumous aggrandizement of Proust would have startled the inhabitants of the Parisian salons of the 1890's, where the young Proust was known as a somewhat effeminate dandy, a young social climber and dilettante, the wastrel son of a famous Catholic doctor and his Jewish wife. But all the time that

Proust, sickly, wan, and seeming to share all the affectations of the gilded youth of the 1890's, was cutting his minor swath through society, he was in fact living a double life. For while he seemed to be existing solely for sensual and snobbish pleasures, he was actually observing the world about him with an intensity and analytical intelligence unmatched, perhaps, since Saint-Simon had observed the court of Louis XIV at Versailles. Without recourse to Zola's ever-open notebook, Proust was recording in his mind the last throes of a society doomed to extinction in World War I.

Gradually the vision began to take shape, and after writing *Jean Santeuil*, an immense trial run that went unpublished during Proust's lifetime and was only discovered after World War II, he embarked on his life's work, the seven-volume *Remembrance of Things Past*. Ill health and an increasingly total commitment to his art made Proust in his later years a hermit, writing propped up in bed in his famous cork-lined room and emerging only rarely, a spectral figure checking on

some detail he intended to use in his novel or drinking a glass of champagne at Maxim's. By sheer force of will, Proust managed to survive his asthma just long enough to complete his novel, although the latter volumes were published only after his death in 1922 and the last volume of all, *The Past Recaptured*, never underwent the extensive revisions to which the earlier volumes had been subjected.

In its staggering bulk, *Remembrance of Things Past* covers many subjects besides the decline of French society in the early years of the twentieth century. It is also an autobiographical novel whose narrator, Marcel, clearly is Proust himself, although nowhere does Proust attribute to him either his own Jewish background or his homosexuality. It is

On the surface, Marcel Proust was no different from the countless other young dilettantes who crowded the salons and ballrooms of Parisian high society. But while living the life of a sybarite he was simultaneously recording the decline of a gilded age. His observations, jotted down in the notebooks at left, became part of his masterpiece, Remembrance of Things Past. *France's foremost woman novelist, Colette, produced her earliest works in collaboration with her first husband. The Claudine novels (on display in poster at right) were semi-autobiographical and ran to four volumes.*

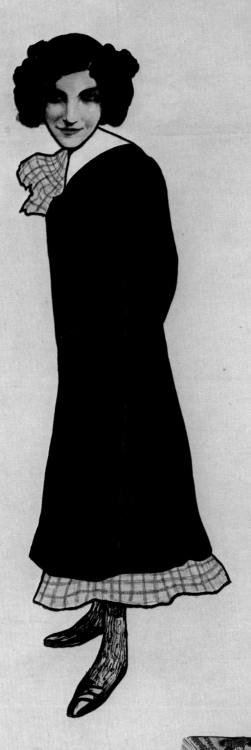

L. LUCIEN FAURE

also, like Wordsworth's *Prelude*, a lyrical account of the "growth of a poet's mind," ending at just that point in Marcel's life when he is about to embark on the writing of the novel that will be *Remembrance of Things Past*.

In addition it is a profound analysis of love—homosexual and heterosexual—of snobbery, of French history, of all the arts, of the psychological processes by which physical objects and experiences evoke the past and by which the past impinges on the present, of all sensual experiences, and of practically everything else under the sun. Yet because of Proust's profound, innate sense of form, *Remembrance of Things Past* is by no means the catch-all this catalogue would suggest, but rather a carefully wrought novel in which all the themes are stated, developed, and refined as in some gigantic symphony by a master composer.

Completely outside the French tradition of terse expression, Proust's prose seems impossibly languorous and involuted to the careless reader; some of his long-winding, but not long-winded, sentences can stretch for pages at a time. But his complexity of style is justified by the complexity of his thought; the difficulty in reading Proust is in tuning in to his infinitely sensitive wavelength, in following the extraordinarily subtle sinuosity of his perceptions about life. Furthermore, he is a great humorist, fully as capable as Dickens of creating robust, larger-than-life comic grotesques, an aspect of him neglected by those readers who find him too precious or decadent for their blunted tastes.

When Proust submitted *Swann's Way*, the first volume of *Remembrance of Things Past*, to the publisher Gallimard, the manuscript was rejected—to the everlasting disgrace of the editor, André Gide. Gide lived to repent his mistake, although his later admiration for Proust always seemed somewhat grudging. Yet in his own way, and during his very long lifetime (1869–1951), Gide's novels had a wider impact on thinking readers than Proust's. He was, in addition, a distinguished essayist, playwright, critic, and Nobel laureate, and it may be that he will be best remembered for the magnificent journals he kept, which are not only an invaluable key to French cultural life in the early twentieth century but are in the grand tradition of personal, moral, and philosophical introspection running from the essays of Montaigne through the journals of the Goncourt brothers and right up to the notebooks of Albert Camus.

As a novelist of the conflict between hedonism and puritanism, between the egoistic individual and an inhibiting society, Gide is in the grand tradition of French clarity and precision of analysis. Pure intelligence perhaps overwhelms pure creativity in his fiction, however, as in the rather overwrought *The Counterfeiters*, a novel about a novelist writing a novel.

Quite the opposite was the great woman writer Colette, whose many volumes of fiction and reminiscences are almost mindless celebrations of the sensual life. Colette has all of Proust's sensuality with little of his analytical intelligence, but her exaltations over the joys of living, ranging from love of flowers and cats to complex love relationships between people, are deeply French in spirit and somewhat analogous to the paintings of the great Impressionists.

The nihilism of Louis-Ferdinand Céline, (below), foreshadowed the "new novelists" of the post-World War II era. But while the existentialism of Albert Camus (above) and Jean-Paul Sartre (shown at right with Simone de Beauvoir) recognized man's lonely condition in an indifferent universe, it also pointed up the individual's freedom to act or not to act, to create his own morality in the absence of predetermined values.

The breakdown of society foreseen by Proust at about the time of World War I elicited many strong novelistic reactions, ranging from François Mauriac's rather dour affirmation of Catholic values to André Malraux's Hemingwayesque celebrations of physical courage and political commitment in *Man's Fate* and *Man's Hope*. These included the nose-thumbing, deliberately irresponsible surrealism of Jean Cocteau and the nihilistic rejection of all social values of Louis-Ferdinand Céline and Henry de Montherlant, the former becoming a Nazi sympathizer, the latter the scourge of modern feminism. The even greater trauma of defeat in World War II produced the existentialist novels of Camus and Sartre and, in the so-called "New Novelists," a rejection of personal introspection in favor of an almost cinematic, hyper-Flaubertian definition of man by means of cataloging his physical surroundings.

Whether the illustrious tradition of the French novel will stifle or encourage future novelists is a moot point. The giant shadow cast by Proust—comparable to that of Joyce in the English-speaking world—and the lure of the movies as a more viable art medium in the twentieth century may indeed leave novelists with nothing new to say in a form so thoroughly explored in France. But at this problematical point in the history of the novel it is still possible that so distinguished a tradition may well produce, by sheer momentum, the geniuses to continue it far into the future.

АЛЕКСАНДРУ СЕРГѢЕВИЧУ
ПУШКИНУ.

4

Russia: the Stifled Heritage

Russia's best-loved poet, Alexander Pushkin (whose grave is seen opposite) was more importantly the creator of Russia's first literary language. What he did for his native land is akin to Dante's achievement in Italy, Chaucer's contribution in England, and Cervantes' in Spain.

COMPARED TO THE LONG HISTORIES of the English and French novels, the Russian novel enjoyed only a brief flowering, with most of its masterpieces coming crowded together in the latter two-thirds of the nineteenth century. Yet so profound an effect have these masterpieces had on readers throughout the world that Russia stands with England, France, and the United States in the vanguard of novel-producing nations. Certainly nowhere else has fiction of such quality been produced under such negative political circumstances. From Pushkin at the beginning of the nineteenth century to Solzhenitsyn in our own time, the Russian literary artist has had to grapple not only with the intractability of his material and the complexity of his art but also with the forces that sought to prevent his being heard at all. And, if anything, the tsarist censorship of the nineteenth century was less oppressive than the Soviet censorship of the twentieth. Indeed, it was under the relatively benign—or at least inefficient—regimes of the later Romanov tsars that the Russian novel enjoyed its brief but spectacular heyday.

But political oppression is only one reason for the relatively recent flowering of the Russian novel. In the seventeenth century, when modern Western ideas of fiction were first beginning to coalesce, the possibilities for creating a realistic literature in Russian were stymied by the polarization of the language itself between Old Church Slavonic, an archaic, highly formalistic language too stiff for any literary purposes beyond theological tracts, and a demotic language that was rich indeed but too rude and uncontrolled for the novel. In the eighteenth century, under Peter I and Catherine II, Russia turned to the West for inspiration in many fields, but in literature it succeeded only in producing pale imitations of Western models. It has indeed been said that modern Russia's peculiar social and political problems stem from the fact that the country never had an age of enlightenment of its own.

In this respect Russia's problem was compounded by the absence of at least one supreme literary figure who had, in the distant past, blended the formal with the colloquial in such a way as to create a living, modern language of sufficient richness and dignity to make a great literature possible. Dante in Italy, Chaucer in England, and Cervantes in Spain had accomplished this necessary task in the late Middle Ages or the Renaissance, but it was not until the nineteenth century that Russia found such a voice in Alexander Pushkin.

It may seem excessive to count the creator of modern literary Russian and the greatest of Russian poets among the ranks of great novelists as well, but in addition to his other feats Pushkin practically invented the Russian short story, a genre in which the Russians have been particularly strong ever since. And while his masterpiece, *Eugene Onegin*, is a lyric narrative poem, it could as easily be considered a novel in verse. So rare is this hybrid form that successful examples of it can literally be counted on the fingers of one hand: Chaucer's *Troilus and Cressida*, Byron's *Don Juan*, Browning's *The Ring and the Book*, Benét's *John Brown's Body*—and, of course, *Eugene Onegin*.

In the romantic, egoistic, destructive eponymous hero of that poem Pushkin created a type derived partly from Hamlet (always a great influence on the Russians), partly from Byron, but mostly from himself, that would dominate the Russian novel throughout the nineteenth century. He is the alienated or superfluous man who can find no purpose in life within the corrupt and moribund society surrounding him, who dissipates his innate gifts of intelligence and sensibility, and who ultimately brings destruction down upon himself and those around him. Later in the century he will become the nihilistic antihero of Dostoevsky and Turgenev; not until the mid-twentieth century will the West really catch up with him.

Pushkin himself was a flamboyant genius who, early in his career, got into trouble with Tsar Alexander I for his liberal poems and his friendship with a number of Decembrists, aristocratic army officers whose December, 1825, revolt was crushed with characteristic ferocity. As a result, Pushkin spent much of his brief life either under house arrest or exiled from his beloved St. Petersburg to the Crimea or the Caucasus. Tsar Nicholas I, Alexander's brother and successor, offered to be Pushkin's personal censor, but no censorship could effectively clip this poet's wings, and with the completion of *Eugene Onegin* in 1833 it became clear to all Russia that the nation's first great poetic voice had been found. He wrote plays as well (*Boris Godunov* is his most famous, in part because of Moussorgsky's great opera based on it), and he penned the first realistic Russian short stories, as opposed to the fantastic folk tales that Russian literature displays in such abundance. Then, in 1837, at the age of thirty-eight, Pushkin was killed in a duel with an army officer over the dubious honor of his wife, Natalia, whom he had married six years earlier. Whether the duel was rigged by the tsar to rid himself of this thorn in his side still remains a mystery, but all Russia mourned the premature death of its greatest poet.

A similar fate overtook Pushkin's most distinguished follower, Mikhail Lermontov, who was killed in a duel when he was only twenty-seven. Lacking Pushkin's vast range and originality, Lermontov nevertheless produced in 1840, the year before his death, one of the great Russian novels, *A Hero of Our Time*, whose romantically doomed hero, Pechorin, recalls Eugene Onegin. Like Pushkin, Lermontov hero-worshiped Byron, was fascinated by the power-figure Napoleon, wrote bawdy and seditious verse that kept him under constant tsarist surveillance (he was arrested for a secretly circulated poem about Pushkin's death), and found inspiration in the wild scenery and folk-

ways of the Caucasus, which he came to know as an army officer fighting tribes of native brigands. In the early nineteenth century, in fact, the Caucasus resembled the American West of a half-century later.

All this experience helped shape *A Hero of Our Time,* which seems at first glance a random collection of short stories loosely connected by the enigmatic central figure of Pechorin but which actually is a highly sophisticated novel involving shifts of time and point of view that would only much later come into general usage as fictional techniques. The title is an ironic comment both on the egoistic nature of Pechorin's heroism and the oppressive times in which such acts of "heroism" as drinking, dueling, womanizing, and playing Russian roulette were the only viable alternatives for a man of spirit and imagination.

With the premature deaths of the great romantics Pushkin and Lermontov, the Russian novel entered a new phase of realism, one that was to mark it ever afterwards. The first great figure of the new epoch was Nikolai Gogol, who began his career with some feeble romantic verse but who eventually found a unique voice of his own, both realistic and fantastic, both comic and demonic, and always deeply original. Equally unsuccessful as a government clerk and a professor of history, Gogol turned to the writing of highly colored short stories of Ukrainian life that made a considerable impression on Pushkin and many others. His comic gifts were first fully explored in a play, *The Inspector General,* one that has held the boards to this day and that seems eternally fresh as a satire on government bureaucracy and small-town cupidity.

Gogol's fictional masterpiece, however, is *Dead Souls,* the first part of which appeared in 1842. One of the supposed truisms of Russian literature, at least in the minds of many Western readers, is that it is oppressively morbid and pessimistic. The title *Dead Souls* would seem to support that view, but nothing could be further from the truth. Although the ultimate vision of Russia in *Dead Souls* is, as Pushkin himself observed, a very sad one, the novel abounds in uproarious good humor and brilliant satiric wit. It is a picaresque novel about the adventures of a small-time swindler named Chichikov as he goes about Russia trying to buy from landowners the names of their dead serfs so he can mortgage them and thus acquire land of his own. The landowners, a stupid, grasping, suspicious lot, don't quite understand why Chichikov wants to buy dead serfs, and the bargaining between them is hilarious as Chichikov journeys through a comic-nightmare Russia of muddy roads, vermin-infested inns, and thieving bureaucrats.

Like *Don Quixote* and *Pickwick Papers, Dead Souls* employs the loose picaresque technique to give a panoramic view of an entire nation at a momentous time in its history. And the times were momentous indeed: the institution of serfdom was doomed—the serfs would be emancipated by 1861—and Russia, like the divided American Union, was undergoing social upheavals of volcanic proportions as a whole way of life disappeared before the writer's eyes. At the end of *Dead Souls* Gogol compares the destiny of Russia to a troika racing headlong into the future. The path this madly lumbering troika should take was of primary concern to the novelists of the nineteenth century and the cause of great divisions among them.

Like his mentor Pushkin, Mikhail Lermontov (left) was to die prematurely in a petty duel—but not before he had completed A Hero of Our Time, *a fine Russian novel that marks the introduction of psychological realism. The comic genius of Nikolai Gogol (above) was at its best in the deft intermingling of realism with fantasy. His noteworthy picaresque novel,* Dead Souls *(title page below), is outrageously funny, offering a glimpse of prerevolutionary Russia that is at once humorous and grotesque.*

When the first part of *Dead Souls* appeared, it was hailed by the influential liberal critic Vissarion Belinsky for what he mistakenly saw as its anatomization of a dead society from a radical point of view. Belinsky stressed the realism of the novel, ignoring its elements of fantasy, and—as he was to do with the young Dostoevsky—he wrongly assumed that Gogol was writing in favor of sweeping social reform. In fact, Gogol became an increasingly fanatical Slavophile, a political reactionary, and a religious zealot.

The issue of the Slavophiles against the Westernizers is of ultimate importance in understanding the Russian novelists of the nineteenth century. At least since the time of Peter the Great (1672–1725) the course of Russian history has veered between the opposite poles of imi-

The depth of Fyodor Dostoevsky's personal suffering is partially revealed in the prison portrait opposite. Sentenced to death for associating with a group of socialists, he received a last-minute reprieve and instead spent four years at hard labor in Siberia. But Dostoevsky was able to redeem his anguish in his art, and his novels have a psychological insight and emotional power unmatched in Russian literature. He was intrigued by violence and obsessed with the duality of good and evil in the human heart, subjects that figure prominently in his fiction.

tation and rejection of the West, a tendency still manifest in Soviet foreign policy. To the Westernizing element in Russia, the country was hopelessly backward in government, science, and technology, and it needed to be modernized according to Western standards. To the Slavophile, this would be a great mistake, as it would only bring to Russia all the ills of modern Western technology with none of the benefits. To them, there was something sacred at the very core of "Holy Russia" that must not be tampered with. Theirs was a mystical apprehension of an inward-looking Russia as the salvation of a world otherwise given over to materialism and godlessness. They found in the woebegone, uneducated serf, tilling the land in complete submission both to master and to God, a figure of infinite wisdom and dignity—far loftier than the supposedly liberated wage slaves of the West.

Although he was certainly conscious of the backwardness of Russia, Gogol relished its peculiar customs and folkways, and although he lived most of his life abroad, in Germany and Italy, he never ceased to think of Russia with intense nostalgia and he never ceased to be concerned about its efforts at modernization. Far from writing *Dead Souls* as a tract for reform, however, he conceived of it as a Russian version of Dante's *Divine Comedy*, tracing the upward course of the soul (Chichikov) from Hell through Purgatory to Heaven. Just before his death he burned the unfinished third part of his masterpiece and much of the second, so that all we have in complete form is the first section, or Hell. Gogol's intention was to show Chichikov's—and Russia's—redemption through complete, self-abnegating acceptance of Christ. Unfortunately, the portions we have of part two are relatively weak, partly because Gogol's satiric genius was more adept at showing the bad than the better, and partly because he suffered from extreme mental disturbance in his last years and was unable to complete his grandiose design.

Gogol's heir, both in his genius for blending the realistic with the fantastic and in his total commitment to an obscurantist, reactionary Slavophilism, was Fyodor Dostoevsky. The peculiar torments of Dostoevsky's life began when his father, a doctor, was murdered by his serfs in 1839, the year Fyodor turned eighteen. Over the next decade Dostoevsky was associated with the liberal Westernizers, but in 1849 he was arrested as part of a socialist discussion group, sentenced to death, and rescued only at the moment of execution by a last-minute decree from the "merciful" tsar, who had never intended to give the young radicals more than a salutary fright. Instead, Dostoevsky was sentenced to four years of hard labor in Siberia.

There he began suffering periodically from the epilepsy that was to haunt his life, and there he started shifting his views to an extreme reactionary position. Although he was strongly influenced by Dickens and other Western writers, a trip to the Great Exhibition in London convinced him that Russia should shun Western material progress and look into its own soul for salvation. In 1861 he wrote *The House of the Dead*, a powerful narrative of his prison experience and the first of what has proved to be a long series of great prison accounts in Russian literature, among them Chekhov's *The Island* and Solzhenitsyn's *One Day in the Life of Ivan Denisovich*.

But the masterpieces we think of as characteristically Dostoevskian began with *Notes from Underground* in 1864, a year grimly marked for the author by the deaths of his brother and his first wife. *Notes from Underground* presents, in its unnamed antihero, the "underground man," the first great vision of hypersensitive, alienated modern man—a man of split personality and self-destructiveness who would ever after be associated with Dostoevsky. As much a bitter diatribe against the glib nineteenth-century faith in progress as it is a novella, *Notes from Underground* presents in clearest expository form Dostoevsky's belief in the necessity for self-abasement and humiliation if mankind is ever to achieve salvation.

This seminal work was followed by *Crime and Punishment*, *The Idiot*, *The Possessed*, and, shortly before Dostoevsky's death in 1881, by his crowning masterpiece, *The Brothers Karamazov*. A murder is at the core of each of these novels, for Dostoevsky shared Dickens's fascination with crime. But unlike Dickens he sees crime in existential, philosophical terms and is far more profound about the mind of the criminal. In *Crime and Punishment*, for example, his hero is a proto-Nietzschean would-be superman; in *The Idiot* he is an epileptic Christ figure returned to earth in the highly un-Christian nineteenth century; in *The Possessed* he is a nihilist, one of an ever-burgeoning breed of political extremists in mid-nineteenth-century Russia whom Dostoevsky at once feared and despised. The nihilists, having despaired of achieving social and political progress through peaceful means, were prepared to commit any crime to overturn the system, and Dostoevsky—fascinated by their criminality, with which he forcefully identified, yet appalled by their radical lack of faith—was obsessed with them.

In *The Brothers Karamazov* his fascination with the schizophrenic personality resulted in a masterfully realized dramatic splitting of the human soul into three component parts, each personified by one of the brothers: Ivan, the agnostic intellectual; Alyosha, the humbly spiritual man of faith; and Dmitri, the man of average sensuality. Like *Dead Souls*, *The Brothers Karamazov* was intended as only the first novel in a trilogy, each novel of which would concentrate on one of the brothers, but death prevented Dostoevsky from completing this grandiose project. As it is, in all its richly realized detail, its psychological incisiveness and philosophical profundity, *The Brothers Karamazov* is hardly a fragment, but rather one of the supreme achievements of world literature.

No two contemporary novelists of comparable stature could be less alike than Dostoevsky and Ivan Turgenev, the "beautiful genius" of Henry James's phrase. Where Dostoevsky stemmed from the lower middle class, Turgenev was an aristocrat; where Dostoevsky was an almost demonically driven man, a compulsive gambler, and a dogmatic reactionary, Turgenev was gentle, poised, and able to see both sides of a question, although temperamentally and intellectually he tended to side with the liberal Westernizers. "I'm a sick man . . . a mean man. There's nothing attractive about me," Dostoevsky's autobiographical underground man truthfully proclaims. Turgenev's tall, handsome body, on the other hand, contained a healthy mind and generous spirit,

Ivan Turgenev (above) could not have been less like his contemporary Dostoevsky. An aristocrat, he grew up on a large estate outside Moscow that may well have resembled the one seen opposite. He was probably Russia's most cosmopolitan novelist, one who numbered Flaubert, Maupassant, Zola, and Henry James among his friends and who was equally at home in Paris, Berlin, Baden, or Moscow.

and his personality is perhaps more attractive to Western readers than that of any other major Russian novelist.

Growing up on a large estate some two hundred miles south of Moscow, Turgenev developed a keen love of nature and a sympathetic affection for the serfs that was balanced by an intense hatred of the institution of serfdom, which he saw at its worst in the hands of a tyrannical, tight-fisted mother who frequently beat him and her serfs alike. Sent to school in Germany, he soon became converted to the Westernizers' cause, and his first literary production, *A Sportsman's Sketches*, aroused tsarist hostility toward him for its sympathetic portrayals of peasant life.

Of all Russian novelists, Turgenev was the most cosmopolitan. Gogol and Dostoevsky had spent many years living away from Russia, but the experience seemed only to intensify their nostalgia for their homeland. Turgenev, touring Europe with Pauline Viardot, a famous opera singer whom he idolized in a curious way (he was also close to her husband), never lost his love for Russia but managed to assimilate the West too, in a way that none of his contemporaries could equal. In the latter part of his career he became a friend of Flaubert, Maupassant, Zola, and James, and he certainly shared the highest ideals of the craft

of fiction with that distinguished circle. Where Dostoevsky was often a crude if powerful writer, Turgenev was never less than polished.

Above all, Turgenev is the poet of the superfluous man, as he no doubt felt himself to be, wandering in the wake of Pauline Viardot from the gambling spa of Baden-Baden (where he helped out the ungrateful Dostoevsky with a loan) to the literary salons of Paris. His heroes almost, but do not quite, make love to his heroines, and both men and women in his novels feel themselves "on the eve" of some great, cataclysmic event that will blast to pieces the monotony of their lives.

Of his major novels—*Rudin*, *On the Eve*, *A Nest of Gentlefolk*, *Smoke*, and *Virgin Soil*—one in particular stands out: *Fathers and Sons*. This may well be the supreme fictional treatment of the generation gap, one in which the aspirations of Russia's liberal youth are pitted against those of the conservative landowning gentry in a conflict of vast social and political, as well as psychological, implications. Centering on Bazarov, a nihilistic young medical student, the novel is a dialectical masterpiece in which both sides of the generation gap are explored with affectionate understanding. For all its fair-mindedness, or perhaps because of it, *Fathers and Sons* aroused a storm of controversy, for both Slavophiles and Westernizers saw themselves traduced in it.

Turgenev found himself at the center of another ugly controversy when the novelist Ivan Goncharov accused him of plagiarizing the older writer's plots. Turgenev was cleared of this charge by a panel of three literary men, but it is nonetheless true that plotting was never his strong point. Indeed, Turgenev's novels work rather as a series of exquisitely perceived character portraits. Indeed, his method was to write extensive biographies of each of his major characters, of which only small portions, like the tip of an iceberg, would finally appear in the finished novel, but every detail of which Turgenev felt he had to have clear in his own mind before composing a novel.

Ironically, Goncharov was even less interested in plotting than was Turgenev. His single masterpiece, *Oblomov*, published in 1859, is an almost completely plotless novel—a triumph of pure stasis in fiction. (The hero spends the first one hundred pages in bed, too lazy to get up and face the world.) *Oblomov* is a great comic novel, one with profound implications, at least for Russian readers, about the more torpid aspects of the Russian soul. Oblomovitis, the spiritual paralysis from which the hero suffers, is a Russian catchword to this day. Lenin once remarked that the Bolshevik Revolution would cure Russia once and for all of Oblomovitis, but it is doubtful that such a deeply perceived national character trait can be expunged by mere revolution.

For many readers, the greatest of Russian novelists is Count Leo Tolstoy. Like Turgenev, he was an aristocrat and a consummate artist, but like Dostoevsky, he was also a man driven to better the world with his spiritual teachings. Tolstoy had so many careers, as soldier, novelist, polemicist, and religious seer, that it would take a volume the length of his own *War and Peace* to begin to come to terms with his protean character. His life and work have the vastness and complexity of Russia itself, and like Russia he was constantly veering between admiration and contempt for the West. Other paradoxes abound in him: a deeply

Count Leo Tolstoy (opposite) is best-known in the West as a novelist, but in Russia he is also recognized as an ethical philosopher and religious reformer. Indeed, he had many careers—and an almost paradoxical personality. But inconsistency and seeming self-contradiction are simply other sides to a man who was truly protean. In his work he captured the vastness of Russia and the diversity of life itself.

Overleaf: *The burning of Moscow in 1812 is but one of many historical events unforgettably described in* War and Peace.

religious man, he was excommunicated by the Orthodox church in 1901; an immensely popular and respected artist, he renounced the art that had produced *War and Peace* and *Anna Karenina* to devote himself to social and religious works; an aristocrat, he dressed and attempted to live like a peasant; an ascetic, he fathered thirteen children and plagued his long-suffering wife with inordinate sexual demands when he was well into his seventies; a brave soldier in the Crimean War, he became a lifelong pacifist; a man of monstrous ego, he denounced the egoism of a Napoleon and cut that romantic figure down to size for all time.

Towering above Tolstoy's many other fine novels, stories, and plays are *War and Peace*, which occupied him from 1863 to 1869, and *Anna Karenina*, which he wrote between 1873 and 1877. For the rest of his long life—he died in 1910 at the age of eighty-two—Tolstoy renounced the art which he had pursued with such consummate skill in favor of setting up schools for peasant children, helping in famine-relief work, raising money to transport the persecuted sect of Dukhobors to Canada (his last major novel, *Resurrection*, was written specifically for that purpose), gathering disciples around him, and fulminating against injustice. Turgenev on his deathbed wrote a letter pleading with Tolstoy to return to his art, but to no avail.

War and Peace began modestly enough in Tolstoy's mind as an account of his ancestors' participation in the 1805 Russian campaign against Napoleon. Gradually it grew through many drafts—each copied out laboriously by the author's wife, Sofya—into one of the longest, as well as greatest, novels ever written. No human activity seems too great or too petty to find its place in the monumental canvas of *War and Peace*, and every element in it, from grand military strategy to middle-class dinners, is treated with profound understanding.

Its two major heroes, Prince Andrew and Pierre, represent two distinct sides of Tolstoy's personality. Prince Andrew is everything urbane, aristocratic, and outgoing in Tolstoy; Pierre is the tortured questioner, the introvert deeply at odds with himself and with society until, through suffering, both marital and martial, he comes to a true vision of man's place in the cosmos. Pitted against the always absorbing private lives of Prince Andrew, Pierre, Natasha, and hundreds of other Russians from tsar to serf, is the ill-fated campaign of Napoleon in Russia, which allows Tolstoy to expound his favorite theories of history, finding the basis for great historical movements in a mystical will of the people rather than in the actions of such "great men" as Napoleon.

No less remarkable an achievement is *Anna Karenina*, in which the doomed, adulterous love of Anna and Vronsky is counterpointed against the search for moral happiness of Levin and Kitty. With all the psychological intelligence Flaubert brought to the analysis of his *Madame Bovary* but with infinitely greater compassion, Tolstoy anatomizes the lovers against the background of a society that can crush them despite the fact that it is morally inferior to them. Many of Tolstoy's later social concerns emerge in Levin, who like Pierre, is searching awkwardly but doggedly for a more meaningful life than the salons of Moscow and St. Petersburg can offer.

With the deaths of the three giants, Dostoevsky, Turgenev, and

Tolstoy, the Russian novel entered what might be called its silver age in the few years remaining before the Bolshevik Revolution was to change fiction as radically as it changed other aspects of Russian life. There were many talented writers in this period but only one outstanding genius—Anton Chekhov. If Chekhov seems a smaller figure than his great predecessors it is only because in his tragically short life—he died at forty-four—he wrote hundreds of short stories and four of the greatest plays in world drama but he was never able to accomplish a full-length novel. His stories, however, are of such quality and influence as to put him among the most important writers of fiction.

Coming from a poverty-stricken family and initially studying medicine as a way out of the slums, Chekhov began while in his early twenties to contribute light sketches and burlesques to magazines in order to augment his pathetically small income. As unpretentious and often crude as these sketches were, they afforded training in an art at which Chekhov was rapidly to became a master. Having noted that medicine was his lawfully wedded wife while literature was his mistress—and adding that he expected to veer between them throughout his life—Chekhov gradually abandoned wife for mistress, to the vast enrichment of the short story as well as the drama.

His great significance in both genres is the way in which he learned to do away with the heavily plotted, "surprise ending" story or play in favor of a seemingly plotless but internally dramatic technique so true to life that it hardly seems to be art. At first reading of a Chekhov story, nothing appears to have happened at all. There are no dramatic confrontations, denouements, or shock effects such as we often find in a story by Maupassant or O. Henry. Yet in each of them a character has been revealed to his inmost core and has come to some terms with himself and with life in a way that makes the story infinitely real and moving—and seemingly unfabricated. Chekhov's technique looks easy to

imitate, but few writers have ever done so with equivalent success. From the vast body of his mature stories emerges a vision of life that is at once sad and comic and always deeply humane—which is precisely what we mean by "Chekhovian."

Chekhov's gentle, ineffectual, self-deluding characters are trapped "between two worlds," as Matthew Arnold stated, "one dead, the other powerless to be born." Shortly after his death in 1904, however, the new world of the Bolshevik Revolution exploded into being, and its effect on the Russian novel is difficult at this point to assess properly.

In the relatively liberal period of the 1920's, experimentation in the arts was encouraged, and for a time Soviet writers were making discoveries about art and fiction that were as exciting as those being made in the West by Joyce, Kafka, or Proust. With Stalin's accession to power, however, Russia entered one of its anti-Western phases, and such experimentalism in the arts was crushed in favor of what Stalinist literary theorists called Socialist Realism—art readily accessible to the lowest common denominator of the public, and art, furthermore, inextricably shackled to propagandistic purposes. Suddenly, there was no room for superfluous men in the Soviet novel.

At far left, the bespectacled Anton Chekhov is shown with Maxim Gorky, the writer who bridged the gap between classical Russia and the new Soviet culture. Although Gorky helped formulate Socialist Realism, Mikhail Sholokov (above) was to prove a far more successful proponent of the genre. The U.S.S.R.'s most important modern writers include Nobel Prize-winners Boris Pasternak (near left) and Alexander Solzhenitsyn (shown at left in the photograph below with author Heinrich Böll).

There were, of course, various possible reactions to this sad state of affairs. Some authors, like the brilliant short-story writer Ivan Bunin and that prodigious master of many languages, Vladimir Nabokov, chose exile or had it imposed on them. Others, like the highly talented short-story writer Isaac Babel, in many ways a Russian Hemingway, simply disappeared, along with so many of his generation, into the yawning maw of the concentration camps, never to be heard from again. Still others produced the hack work demanded by the regime, and as a result Russian literature, which had once boasted a Pushkin and a Chekhov, degenerated into the mass production of agitprop trash about love-in-the-tractor-factory. A very few, among them Mikhail Sholokhov in his novels about the Don Cossacks, *And Quiet Flows the Don* and *The Don Flows Home to the Sea*, were able to merge, more or less successfully, the claims of art with those of Socialist Realism.

Yet the long-term effect of closing Russia to the influences of modern Western art has beeen deeply injurious to the Soviet novel, even at its best. Both Boris Pasternak's *Doctor Zhivago* and the novels of Alexander Solzhenitsyn seem oddly fossilized to Western readers accustomed to such innovative novelists as Joyce and Faulkner. Pasternak and Solzhenitsyn appear to be writing in the realistic tradition of Tolstoy at a time when the best fiction has gone beyond realism. Not that Tolstoy is a bad example for anyone to follow, but to be writing a Tolstoyan novel a century after *War and Peace* is rather like composing a Brahmsian symphony after Bartók; the time is out of joint with the technique. Neither a Brahms nor a Tolstoy can ever really be successfully imitated, least of all long after their deaths in a world very different from the one they graced. The richness of the Russian language and the great heritage of the Russian novelists can never really be submerged for very long, however. Given only a modicum of political freedom—as little even as was enjoyed under the nineteenth-century tsars—the Russian novel is sure to spring into new life.

5

Native Sons

THE AMERICAN NOVEL, oddly enough, more closely resembles the Russian than the English novel—a consequence of its late nineteenth-century flowering, its embodiment of a vast, untamed land of agrarian pioneers, and its tendency toward the fantastic, the mythic, and the metaphysical rather than the reasonable and the socially ordered. Americans, as critic Richard Chase has noted, tend to write romances rather than what are ordinarily conceived of as novels. What Englishman, for instance, would dream of writing, like Melville, a novel about a whale—or, like Faulkner, a novella about a bear?

In his 1879 study of Hawthorne, Henry James set forth in classic terms the dilemma facing the American novelist, at least in the nineteenth century. In contrast to Europe, James maintained, America afforded her would-be novelists:

> No sovereign, no court, no personal loyalty, no aristocracy, no church, no clergy, no army, no diplomatic service, no country gentlemen, no palaces, no castles, nor manors, nor old country houses, nor parsonages, not thatched cottages, nor ivied ruins; no cathedrals, nor abbeys, nor little Norman churches; no great universities nor public schools . . . no literature, no novels, no museums, no pictures, no political society, no sporting class—no Epsom or Ascots! Some such list as that might be drawn up of the absent things in American life . . . the effect of which, upon an English or a French imagination, would probably as a general thing be appalling.

James, who considered a settled tradition essential for the art of fiction, escaped to Europe, where he lived most of his productive adult life. Other American novelists stayed at home and somehow made do with the skimpy social materials at hand, neglecting the novel drawn from a richly complex and stratified society in favor of highly poetic romances derived from their own innermost spiritual beings. In a sense, a novelist like Melville, staying at home, was more of an inner émigré than James, self-exiled to England.

A further problem facing the American novelist, one reminiscent of the plight of the Russians, was the slow development of a native literary language independent of British English. Literary emancipation took much longer to achieve than political emancipation; the Declaration of Independence, for instance, is written in highly formal, eight-

"In wildness is the preservation of the world," proclaimed Henry David Thoreau—and, indeed, civilization versus nature was to become a major nineteenth-century theme in all the arts. Asher B. Durand's Kindred Spirits *(opposite) was commissioned as a memorial to landscape painter Thomas Cole. It commemorates both the friendship and the artistic affinity of Cole, seen on the right, and poet William Cullen Bryant, left.*

eenth-century British English that is useless for the novelist seeking to capture the peculiarities of the native American idiom. The first American novelists, therefore, were heavily influenced—both in their styles and their subject matter—by models from the mother country. Charles Brockden Brown (1771–1810) wrote Gothic romances in the manner of Ann Radcliffe, of which only one, *Wieland*, is considered readable today. The more important James Fenimore Cooper began writing novels in disastrous imitation of Jane Austen's social comedies, but he then went on to ape rather more successfully the historical romances of Sir Walter Scott.

Cooper was the first American novelist to enjoy a widespread reputation in Europe, which was entranced with his accounts of Indian life in the New World, accounts much more convincing than Chateaubriand's sentimental *Atala* and *René* had been. (It is noteworthy in this regard that the last, deathbed scrawl of the great Austrian composer Franz Schubert was a note urging a friend to bring him the latest Cooper novel.) But Cooper's importance goes beyond furnishing romantic Europe with exotic local lore. For although his plots lumber awkwardly, his characters are often little more than stick figures, and his dialogue is unendurably pretentious and inaccurate, this aristocratic gentleman farmer of Cooperstown, New York, somehow discovered and exploited one of the most powerful myths in American literature.

Of Cooper's thirty-four novels, it is the five so-called Leatherstocking Tales that best embody this myth, and it is they that have endured (although Cooper also wrote some splendid sea stories, much admired by such old salts as Melville and Conrad). In order of composition, but not in order of plot chronology, the Leatherstocking Tales are: *The Pioneers, The Last of the Mohicans, The Prairie, The Pathfinder,* and *The Deerslayer.* They detail the adventures of Natty Bumppo, an individualistic man of the woods, expert hunter, friend of the Indians, and hater of the ever-encroaching civilization he encounters in his long life in nature. In his crude way, Cooper first realized the epic potentialities of the restless, self-reliant American pioneer who had turned his back on bourgeois civilization for life on a rapidly receding frontier.

Natty Bumppo resembles such actual American frontier heroes as Daniel Boone, and his conception was to influence both Thoreau, who proclaimed that "in wildness is the preservation of the world," and Mark Twain, who poked glorious fun at Cooper's stylistic inadequacies but who nevertheless ended his masterpiece, *The Adventures of Huckleberry Finn,* with Huck's very Cooperian resolution: "I reckon I got to light out for the Territories ahead of the rest, because Aunt Sally she's going to adopt me and sivilize me, and I can't stand it. I been there before." And even well into the twentieth century we find Cooper's archetypal American in Hemingway's Nick Adams, venturing forth alone to fish the Big Two-Hearted River, and in Faulkner's Isaac McCaslin, who undergoes his rites of passage into manhood on a bear hunt in what remains of the Mississippi woods.

The critic Philip Rahv once divided all American authors into Palefaces and Redskins. In many ways—though not in all—Cooper was the first Redskin; Poe and Hawthorne, the first Palefaces. Neither of the

In Natty Bumppo, of the Leatherstocking Tales, James Fenimore Cooper (above) was to create an archetypal American hero, one who would endure well into the twentieth century. Edgar Allen Poe (far right), on the other hand, was utterly uninterested in the self-reliant pioneer who turns his back on civilization. He set most of his works in Europe, yet with stories such as "The Murders in the Rue Morgue" and "The Black Cat" (both are illustrated at right by Aubrey Beardsley) he established a genuine Gothic tradition in American fiction.

latter was interested in the westward expansion of his country; both wrote fairly standard British English in disregard of the native idiom springing up about them. Poe, who spent only two years of his childhood in England, set most of his stories in Europe, albeit in a fantastic Europe of his imagination. Yet both were great innovators and established a genuine Gothic tradition in American fiction, one that was independent of the rather mechanical and limited Gothicism of European romanticism and at least as important to the American novel as the Redskin tradition of respect for nature and contempt for civilization. With "The Murders in the Rue Morgue" in 1841, Poe also invented the detective story, but his major achievement, apart from his poetry and criticism, lay in such morbid, neurotic tales as "The Fall of the House of Usher" and "The Black Cat." There he was able to encapsulate in art his own personality—often verging on the psychotic—in such a way as to give the Gothic tradition a new life and authenticity. Probing inner psychological horrors rather than manufacturing the stagy, exterior horrors of a Radcliffe, Poe established a tradition that would later prove especially fruitful in the hands of such southern novelists as Faulkner, Capote, and Styron.

Herman Melville, perceiving a "great power of blackness" in Hawthorne's "intricate, profound heart," could just as easily have been referring to Poe—or to himself. All three authors are concerned with psychological and moral horror that is directly at odds with such American yea-sayers as Emerson and Whitman. Poe particularly seems so out of step with the assertive, positivist pre-Civil War American spirit that it is hardly surprising he was neglected during his short, harrowing lifetime and found his greatest admirers in Europe, particularly in France, where he influenced Baudelaire and the symbolist movement in poetry. Given his penchant for an almost melodramatic vulgarity at times, it may be cruel but fair to say that he reads better in translation.

Nathaniel Hawthorne seems a more provincial writer, but a writer better grounded in reality—especially the reality of Puritan New England, where one of his ancestors had been a judge at the Salem witch trials. Like Poe, he was a solitary, haunted man, although his inner loneliness did not drive him to drink and despair as Poe's had done. He

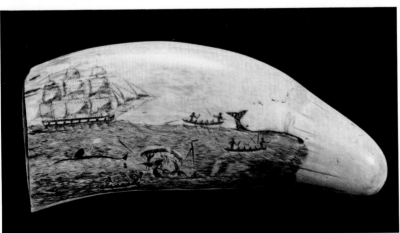

Nathaniel Hawthorne (opposite) was profoundly influenced by his Puritan heritage, and the perpetual combat between good and evil is a recurring motif in his fiction. Hawthorne's use of symbol and allegory was deeply to affect countless American writers, among them his contemporary Herman Melville (above). The latter was to draw heavily on his whaling experiences aboard the Acushnet *(depicted in watercolor at left; below, a similar whaling scene on scrimshaw) for his masterpiece,* Moby Dick—*which he dedicated to Nathaniel Hawthorne.*

knew the major New England Transcendentalists—Emerson, Thoreau, the Alcotts—but he could not share their essential optimism and liberal faith in the potentialities of the new American democratic man. Instead his imagination often withdrew to the haunted Puritan past, which he revivified in numerous short stories as well as in his masterful novels, *The Scarlet Letter* and *The House of the Seven Gables*. All his major fiction is deeply mysterious and allegorical, for he is more interested in dramatizing the inner moral and psychological secrets of the human heart than in rendering realistically the surface of American life. The conflicts between sensual instinct and intellectual or theological repression, between innate evil and glib social and political positivism, give his austere moral fables their unique tension.

In his famous review of *The House of the Seven Gables*, Herman Melville says, "There is the grand truth about Nathaniel Hawthorne. He says No! in thunder; but the Devil himself cannot make him say *yes*. For all men who say *yes*, lie." Melville is absolutely right in this. Indeed, one of the peculiar glories of American literature is that many of its finest novelists are nay-sayers, dead set in their opposition to the semiofficial national dogma of inevitable salvation through material prosperity. Hawthorne was born on the Fourth of July, but it would be difficult to find a novelist less concerned with celebrating mere political independence—not when man, at least in Hawthorne's eyes, was still shackled to his propensities for evil.

Melville, too, was one of the great loners of American literature. Born into a comfortably prosperous New York family, he went to sea as a young man but deserted ship in the Marquesas Islands. His experience with the "noble savages" of the South Seas produced his early, heavily autobiographical novels, *Typee* and *Omoo*, the only real successes he enjoyed in his lifetime. Stereotyped as an exotic travel writer, Melville found himself losing his audience when he wrote more difficult, complex novels like *Moby Dick*, *Mardi*, and *Pierre*—novels in which the element of adventure was clearly subordinate to dark philosophizing about man's evil and God's indifference. *Moby Dick*, he admitted, was "broiled in hell fire," and so original in concept, so poetic in treatment, that it baffled readers seeking nothing more than a good sea yarn. Melville spent the last forty years of his life trying unsuccessfully to recapture a vanished audience while refusing to compromise with the debased contemporary taste for sentimental fiction.

Only since the 1930's, in fact, has Melville's supreme significance in American fiction been generally recognized, and only since that time has Captain Ahab's relentless pursuit of the great white whale been seen as the rich poetic allegory it is. Many fathoms below the surface of Melville's adventure story is a profound exploration of man's eternal struggle with an implacable, uncaring nature and with the evil residing in his own soul—and that aspect, too, has only recently been properly plumbed. If ever a writer had to wait until long after he was dead for the times to catch up with his prophetic vision, Melville is that writer.

If Melville's career was tragically aborted by lack of popular recognition, precisely the opposite can be said of the career of Mark Twain, whose worldwide popularity seriously eroded his artistic talents. In his important essay, "Hawthorne and His Mosses," Melville asserted that "no American writer should write like an Englishman, or a Frenchman; let him write like a man, for then he will be sure to write like an American. Let us away with this [Bostonian] leaven of literary flunkyism towards England." Yet it was neither Hawthorne nor Melville who achieved a purely American prose style. That was the exclusive triumph of Mark Twain, whom his friend William Dean Howells—critic, editor of the *Atlantic*, and no mean novelist himself—dubbed "the Lincoln of our literature." As Lincoln liberated the slaves, so did Twain liberate, for all time, American writing from British English.

Growing up in Hannibal, Missouri, far from the New England literary establishment, and serving as small-town newspaper editor, Mississippi River pilot, and prospector in Nevada, Samuel Clemens picked up and used, as no American novelist before him had done, the pungently expressive vernacular of American speech. Ernest Hemingway acknowledged this feat in *Green Hills of Africa*: "All modern American literature comes from one book by Mark Twain called *Huckleberry Finn* . . . it's the best book we've had. All American writing comes from that. There was nothing before. There has been nothing as good since."

Yet in Twain's immense popularity as a frontier humorist and

Called by William Dean Howells "the Lincoln of our literature," Mark Twain is universally recognized as the liberator of American prose, long oppressed by British English. Indeed, his humor was as distinctly American as the idiomatic dialogue he used in his novels and stories. Twain's vision was to darken as he aged, however, and the white flannel suits he affected in his later years (opposite) were in sharp contrast to the pessimism and misanthropy of such works as The Mysterious Stranger.

after-dinner speaker, in his pursuit of wealth, often by harebrained business schemes, he never quite fully developed as an artist in fiction. The total vision of Twain is what is important; no single novel is a perfect work of art, and even *The Adventures of Huckleberry Finn* degenerates in its last hundred pages into aimless burlesque.

Twain was an instinctive artist in prose, however, incapable of writing a dull sentence or paragraph. His problems came in organizing a work as long as a novel and from a tendency to take easy recourse to his infinite fund of humor when the purely fictive going got rough. Because he was early typed as a writer of boys' books—a reputation such works as *The Adventures of Tom Sawyer* and *A Connecticut Yankee in King Arthur's Court* support—readers of Mark Twain were long unconscious of a deep strain of pessimism in him that was as black in its own way as the visions of Poe, Hawthorne, and Melville. It even appears in the sunlit *Huckleberry Finn*, particularly when Huck and his companion, the runaway slave Jim, leave their raft and the idyllic freedom of the Mississippi to encounter what passed for human society at that time. Clearly the frontier violence young Sam Clemens had seen left a deep mark on him, one that his literary reputation in the East and his marriage to the rather proper Olivia Langdon could never efface.

The Mississippi (seen in a Currier and Ives lithograph below) was to have a pervasive influence on Twain's life as well as on his art. It was to give him his pen name—"Mark Twain" being river jargon for two fathoms deep—and also provide him with vivid experiences that he later incorporated into such classics as The Adventures of Huckleberry Finn *and* Tom Sawyer.

With the death of his favorite daughter, Susy, in 1896 and of Olivia in 1904, Twain's vision grew ever darker, so that such late works as *The Mysterious Stranger*, while still on the surface "boys' books," seethe with ferocious contempt for what Twain called "the damned human race." If Twain sometimes resembles an American Dickens in his flamboyance, popularity, and humor, his pessimism and savage indignation make him even closer to an American Swift.

In the figure of Tom Sawyer, Twain vested all his propensities for nostalgic, romantic fantasizing about idyllic youth, as well as his yearning for adult respectability. But he gave the more important part of himself to Huck Finn—the outcast from prim, stuffy society, the self-reliant frontiersman, the seemingly naïve and uneducated but deeply perceptive critic of the mores of bourgeois white America on the eve of the Civil War.

That conflict itself failed to produce an American *War and Peace*, as some writers and critics thought it would or should. Most of the literary giants of the time, men like Hawthorne and Melville, sat on the sidelines both physically and spiritually, despising the self-righteous cant on both sides. Twain enlisted briefly and ingloriously in the Confederate Army and then wrote a hilarious sketch about his misadventures. Yet a novel written by Harriet Beecher Stowe, *Uncle Tom's Cabin*, published in 1851, the same year as *Moby Dick*, had a profound impact on American attitudes toward slavery—so much so that when President Lincoln invited Mrs. Stowe to the White House he greeted her with the words, "So you're the little woman who wrote the book that made this great war." Never has a novel been so directly influential on so great a political event as *Uncle Tom's Cabin* was on the Civil War. It remains the most important of all propaganda novels, but most modern readers find Mrs. Stowe's lengthy work ludicrously sentimental, melodramatic, and amateurishly written in slavish imitation of Dickens at his worst.

The war itself was to find perhaps its best fictional treatment thirty years after it ended—in *The Red Badge of Courage*, written by a twenty-four-year-old New Jersey newspaperman named Stephen Crane. Crane did not experience any war at all until 1896—the year after *The Red Badge of Courage* was published—when he covered an insurrection in Cuba. Nonetheless, his short account of Private Henry Fleming's ordeal at what was probably the 1863 battle of Chancellorsville remains a classic of war writing; it is matched in American fiction only by Hemingway's *A Farewell to Arms*—as spiritually resonant, for all its brevity, as the war writing in Tolstoy. Crane's death from tuberculosis in 1900 cut tragically short what would have been a major novelistic career.

It was Twain who gave the period of American life just after the war its name. He called it "the Gilded Age," after the title of a novel he wrote in collaboration with Charles Dudley Warner. Like all of Twain's novels, this one was artistically very uneven, but it did brilliantly satirize—in the career of its raffish hero, Colonel Sellers—the very sort of ill-advised dabbling in business ventures that had managed to drain away almost all the fortune Twain's books had earned him.

The business ethic of the time was rather more successfully cap-

tured by William Dean Howells in such novels as *The Rise of Silas Lapham* and *A Hazard of New Fortunes*. Howells's concentration on what he himself rather unfortunately called "the smiling aspects" of American life has prevented future generations from doing appropriate justice to a master realist. His vision, like Twain's, darkened progressively before the greed and rapacity of the Gilded Age, until this Ohio farm boy who had come to Boston to make his literary fortune and win respectability ended up a Tolstoyan socialist speaking out against injustices wherever he found them.

Howells's other great friend, Henry James, was as different from Mark Twain as Turgenev was different from Dostoevsky; Howells's friendship with both must have been a miracle of tact and generosity of spirit. Twain looked west for inspiration, James looked east. Where Twain was an almost complete Redskin, James was the quintessential Paleface. Where Twain was a slovenly artist in fiction, James, a friend and disciple of Flaubert and Turgenev, in his 22 novels, 112 short stories, and innumerable pieces of criticism was both the greatest American theorist and practitioner of the art of fiction. Where Twain reveled in being "an innocent abroad," James was a born sophisticate, whether in the literary salons of Paris, the aristocratic stately homes of England, or—far more rarely—in Newport, Boston, or his native New

In 1851, Harriet Beecher Stowe (above) created a sensation with her first novel, Uncle Tom's Cabin. Its attack on the institution of slavery (benignly depicted at left) polarized public opinion and contributed directly to the outbreak of the American Civil War. The most masterful piece of war writing to come out of that conflict was Stephen Crane's The Red Badge of Courage, a fictionalized account of Private Henry Fleming's ordeal at Chancellorsville (below).

York. Where Twain was an enormous success with the public from the instant he set pen to paper, James, almost like Melville, remained largely unrecognized until relatively recent times, when he gained a reputation as the greatest American novelist of the nineteenth century and perhaps of ours as well.

The younger brother of William James—the famous psychologist and author of *The Varieties of Religious Experience*—Henry was born into a comfortable literary milieu in New York City, the son of the eccentric philosopher Henry James, Sr., whose intimacy with the literary great men of the age brought Henry, Jr., an avuncular pat on the head from no less than Thackeray when he was on an American tour. As a boy, Henry was frequently trundled off to Europe for extended periods of time, and although on his return to America he made desultory attempts to study art and law it became clear by his mid-twenties that he was destined for the literary life. An "obscure hurt" suffered while fighting a fire in Newport in 1861 made him ineligible for service in the Civil War and further consigned him to the sedentary life of authorship. After several transatlantic trips he eventually settled down in London in the 1880's. He returned to the United States only once, in 1905, and ultimately, shortly before his death in 1916, he became a naturalized British subject.

The interplay of the American and European characters, cultures, and attitudes toward life thus formed a major subject for James's fiction, works in which he studied with extraordinary subtlety and sensitivity either Americans in Europe ("Daisy Miller," *The American, The Ambassadors*) or, more rarely, Europeans in America (*The Europeans*). Some of his novels deal purely with English life (*What Maisie Knew, The Princess Casamassima*); others exclusively with American (*Washington Square, The Bostonians*). In the conflict of values arising from juxtaposed cultures, however, James was best able to come to grips with what he called "the complex fate" of being an American.

But what James called his "international theme" was only one of many central concerns in his fiction. Another is the role of the artist or writer in a materialistic society. Another is the way the past haunts the present, for, like Poe, James was a master of the true Gothic of psychological horror. Still another is the ambiguous interplay between innocence and evil, which concerned Hawthorne and Melville too, but which James treats in a more richly realistic and psychologically penetrating way. He is, in Joseph Conrad's perceptive phrase, "the historian of fine consciences."

And all the time, in letters and notebooks, in literary journalism and in the great prefaces to the New York edition of his collected novels and tales, James was bringing to the theory and criticism of the art of fiction the finest aesthetic intelligence of any American novelist. The most self-conscious of all novelists, James always knew exactly what he was doing and how best to dramatize his themes within a keenly apprehended metaphysic of the novel.

It has been noted that there were three major periods in James's work, wittily dubbed James I, James II, and The Old Pretender. The style of James I, best seen in "Daisy Miller" and *Washington Square*, is

light, urbane, and pellucid. With James II, social high comedy tends to give way to deeper moral concerns and a more daringly idiosyncratic prose. The masterpiece of this period—and perhaps of James's whole career—is *The Portrait of a Lady*. The really difficult James is The Old Pretender, who reigned during the first years of the twentieth century and produced three supreme triumphs: *The Wings of the Dove*, *The Ambassadors*, and *The Golden Bowl*. Here the style is so clotted and involuted, the dialogue so cryptic and allusive, the psychologizing and moralizing so infinitely subtle, the characters' sensibilities so mandarin as to constitute a major pitfall for the lazy or careless reader. Amazingly, these dense late novels were all dictated to a secretary.

As with Proust, however, the stylistic difficulties of late James are not designed to baffle or irritate but rather to render as realistically and clearly as possible the coruscations of an infinitely complex mind. Late James is like late Beethoven, who also had three major, discernible periods of creativity. Beethoven's last string quartets offer difficulties and may seem perversely complicated to the listener who knows only his earlier symphonies, but they are the quintessential refinement, after a lifetime's struggle with musical thought, of a wise, totally mature, and deeply humane master.

Similarly, a novel like *The Golden Bowl* is the master's ultimately distilled final statement of both the international theme and the theme of the symbiotic relationship between moral predator and victim, between spiritual innocence and selfish betrayal, that had obsessed James all his life and that, in his last years, he was able to shape into novels of uttermost complexity and beauty, revealing these qualities only to the most alert and sensitive of readers. With this shy, generous, rather fussy Anglophile bachelor, wholly devoted to his art, the American novel attained its loftiest peak of perfection.

If Mark Twain was "an innocent abroad," Henry James was probably America's most sophisticated and cosmopolitan literary ambassador. James spent most of his adult life in Europe, and he eventually became a British subject. Nevertheless, his art was unquestionably American, dealing with such mature themes as the plight of the artist in society and innocence versus experience, particularly in the confrontation between European and American civilizations. One of James's most difficult works, The Golden Bowl *(the frontispiece from the New York edition is shown at left), was written late in the master craftsman's career. Its flawless technique marks the pinnacle of James's art.*

6

The American Century

Ours has frequently been called "the American century," and never more accurately than in reference to the history of the novel. For with complete liberation from English models and a veritable explosion of native talent, the American novel has won worldwide prestige in less than eight decades.

Interestingly enough, it is possible to pinpoint the exact date when the twentieth century began for American fiction. On November 8, 1900, the firm of Doubleday, Page grudgingly published *Sister Carrie*, the first novel of Theodore Dreiser. Although it was on the whole well reviewed, *Sister Carrie* sold only about five hundred copies of its first printing, which according to legend was semisuppressed on "moral" grounds by the publisher's wife and which won its strange, lumbering author not royalties but a nervous breakdown.

At first glance, Dreiser seems to be merely an American Zola in his dogged application of "scientific method" to the pursuit of naturalism, in his sense of an overriding genetic and economic determinism governing the usually blighted lives of his characters, in his social and political commitments—and in his lack of literary style. Yet Dreiser is a far more significant figure in American fiction than Zola is in French. He is, as Ellen Moers has claimed in the finest critical work on Dreiser, "a great novelist, perhaps the greatest of the Americans." And this in spite of a prose style so painfully awkward, humorless, insensitive, and cliché ridden that it seems at times almost embarrassingly amateurish.

The most significant biographical fact about Dreiser is that he was the first major American author who was not born of middle-class British Protestant stock. Instead, he was born into a wretchedly poor, semi-literate German Catholic family in Terre Haute, Indiana, where German was spoken at home more frequently than English and where Dreiser was one of ten children. He escaped this sordid and stifling milieu to become a newspaperman in Chicago and St. Louis, and he ultimately drifted to New York, where his older brother Paul Dreiser was making a hit on Tin-pan Alley with such songs as "My Gal Sal" and "On the Banks of the Wabash."

It wasn't until 1911 that Dreiser recuperated sufficiently from the disastrous debut of *Sister Carrie* to write a second novel, *Jennie Gerhardt*, and during those years he supported himself as a hack journalist and editor of a variety of women's magazines. But *Jennie Gerhardt* led

Childe Hassam's nostalgic painting of Washington Square Arch evokes the graciousness of post-Civil War New York. It was against such a backdrop that Edith Wharton set The Age of Innocence, *but unlike Hassam she probed beneath the city's idyllic façade to expose a society fossilized by convention and ill-equipped to meet the demands of the twentieth century.*

103

quickly to *The Financier*, the first novel in his so-called "trilogy of desire," which dealt with the spectacular career of Frank Cowperwood, a typical robber baron of the turn of the century.

In 1925 Dreiser produced his masterpiece, the massively impressive *An American Tragedy*. By this time—thanks largely to the tireless propagandizing on his behalf by the influential maverick critic H.L. Mencken and by others concerned with a realistic approach to the problems of American life—Dreiser's fame had become secure. He was seen as the most powerful and effective destroyer of the genteel tradition that had dominated popular American fiction in the post-Civil War period, spreading its soft blanket of provincial, sentimental romance over the often ugly realities of life in modern, industrialized, urban America. Certainly there was nothing genteel about Dreiser, either as man or novelist. He was the supreme poet of the squalid, a man who felt the terror, the pity, and the beauty underlying the American dream. With an eye at once ruthless and compassionate, he saw the tragedy inherent in the American success ethic; the soft underbelly, as

The affluence and gentility into which Edith Wharton (right) was born contrasted sharply with the humble origins of Theodore Dreiser (above), one of ten children born to indigent German parents in Terre Haute, Indiana. The raw realism of Dreiser and artists such as George Bellows (represented by the lithograph at left) was continents apart from Wharton's world of impeccable manners and inherited wealth. Nevertheless, her satiric eye delineated a society that was as stifling, albeit not as predatory, as Dreiser's capitalistic jungle.

it were, of the Horatio Alger rags-to-riches myth so appealing to the optimistic American imagination.

The heroine of *Sister Carrie* does indeed succeed—in the theater— because of her irrepressible vitality. At the same time, and in grim counterpoint, her lover Hurstwood descends just as inexorably from his once mighty position as manager of a glittering Chicago saloon to the Bowery, where his last words as he turns on the gas in a flophouse are "What's the use?" Similarly, Clyde Griffiths of *An American Tragedy* ends up in the electric chair for murdering the pregnant sweetheart who stood in the way of his rise to material success. This latter book was based on an actual murder case, but Dreiser never had to look far to find documentary evidence to support his indictment of the Darwinian power struggle going on in the jungle of American capitalism. Moreover, his vision has troubled the American imagination ever since, both in the crudely naturalistic Chicago novels of James T. Farrell and in the more elegantly conceived works of F. Scott Fitzgerald and Nathanael West.

Indeed, not all fictional renditions of life in the big city were as stark and raw as Dreiser's. The New York in which Hurstwood meets his sordid end seems a thousand miles removed from the "little old New York" of Edith Wharton, friend—and to a certain extent disciple—of Henry James. Here, graciousness and a strict, often snobbish, but essentially supportive social and moral code mark the lives of the Four Hundred, who dominated the New York society into which Edith Newbold Jones was born in 1862. Here is a cozy, rather provincial world of assured, inherited wealth and good manners in which Mrs. Wharton's characters move, but here too a social or moral misstep can lead to disaster, as it does for Lily Bart, the haunting heroine of Wharton's first important novel, *The House of Mirth*, for Lily, no less than Hurstwood, is hounded to death by a relentlessly materialistic, unforgiving society. Later, in the Pulitzer Prize-winning *The Age of Innocence*, Edith Wharton could look back on her world with a certain nostalgia from the elegant country house in France where she had exiled herself. Increasingly repulsed by the collapse of morals and manners following World War I, she could occasionally show her bitterness, as she did in *The Custom of the Country*, but *The Age of Innocence* remains an almost pastoral evocation of a fossilized urban way of life at once admirable and woefully ill-equipped to resist the onslaught of post-Civil War "new money" and the concomitant breakdown in public and private morals.

Willa Cather (above) drew on her own Nebraska childhood for her regional novels of immigrant settlers' life on the Great Plains. O Pioneers! *was followed by* Song of the Lark *and the moving* My Antonia, *two scenes from which are depicted below. America's frontier farmlands were also to inspire Thomas Hart Benton, whose bucolic* Cradling Wheat *(above, right) is imbued with the fecundity and bounty of the prairie.*

Even more idyllic than Wharton's visions, and almost totally lacking her satiric bite, was Willa Cather's view of the lost world of her girlhood, the prairies of Nebraska. In a sense, Willa Cather is a regionalist, doing for Nebraska what the older Sarah Orne Jewett had done for Maine in *The Country of the Pointed Firs*. But beyond the celebration of a particular region, beyond mere local color, Willa Cather, like Edith Wharton, was nostalgically evoking a simpler way of life and tracing its downfall at the hands of civilization. Distant though New York may be from Nebraska, both women found similar virtues in their aboriginal inhabitants.

Cather's heroes are the pioneers who settled the Middle West against the almost overwhelming forces of an implacable nature, only to find their finest qualities of cooperation and endurance being dissipated in following generations by crass materialism. Her finest novels are *O Pioneers!*, *The Song of the Lark*, *My Antonia*, and *The Professor's House*, and they are all written in a luminous prose as carefully fashioned as Dreiser's is clumsy and careless. They are all imbued with an almost Virgilian celebration of the heroic and with an intense nostalgia for a lost past, which is sometimes sentimentalized while the present is bitterly traduced.

Equally important in opening up the Midwest as material for American fiction were Sherwood Anderson of Ohio and Sinclair Lewis of Minnesota, both of whom had a horror of what Lewis was to call "the village virus." Anderson, the older of the two, simply walked off his job in an Ohio paint factory one day to become a highly influential short-story writer and novelist. Indeed, his masterpiece, *Winesburg, Ohio*, is at the same time a collection of short stories and a coherent novel stressing the loneliness and frustrations of sensitive souls caught in a web of small-town pettiness, gossip, and conformity. His prose is as

limpid and colloquial as Willa Cather's, but in his later works it becomes so mannered and sentimental as almost to parody itself.

Winesburg, Ohio came out in 1919—heralding the new spirit that would permeate American fiction in the 1920's. The year 1920 itself was a magic year for the novel, marking as it did the publication of Wharton's *The Age of Innocence*, F. Scott Fitzgerald's epochal *This Side of Paradise*, and Sinclair Lewis's *Main Street*. Like Anderson, Lewis rebelled against the conformities and cultural deprivations of the American small town in the early years of the twentieth century, but where Anderson was at his best stressing the effect of such a restricted environment on his alienated heroes, Lewis's greatest gift was the satiric mimicking of the speech patterns and absurdly provincial mores of the majority. True, Carol Kennicott, the heroine of *Main Street*, is a sort of transplanted Emma Bovary in her romantic rebellion against stifling Gopher Prairie, but Lewis's facile, disorganized talent functions best when he is gravely rendering the bourgeois fatuities of the self-important businessmen, the Rotarians, and the joiners with whom Carol futilely struggles.

In *Babbitt*, which many consider his masterpiece, Lewis so successfully realized this type that he gave a new word to the American language. *Dodsworth*, a later attempt to give a fairer, better-balanced portrait of an American businessman, was less successful, as was *Arrowsmith* in portraying an idealistic doctor. But when Lewis could give full vent to his immense satiric gifts, as in the savage *Elmer Gantry*, a Tartuffian portrait of a religious humbug, he displayed a truly impressive talent for that favorite 1920's occupation, debunking.

Indeed, America in the twenties was a place most of its writers deplored and were eager to escape from. World War I itself had been a sufficiently disillusioning experience—not for Americans alone—and it directly inspired such splendid novels as E. E. Cummings's account of his imprisonment in France, *The Enormous Room*, John Dos Passos' *Three Soldiers*, and Ernest Hemingway's *A Farewell to Arms*. But in a way the ambience of postwar America was even more disillusioning, especially to those writers who had come back from the war to find a world made safe not so much for democracy as for mediocrity, Prohibition, and Babbitry. Whereas Henry James had been an almost unique exile to Europe in the 1880's, the 1920's saw boatloads of American writers heading for France, where they could live cheaply, drink to their hearts' content, write as they pleased, and laugh together at the fatuities and corruptions of the Harding, Coolidge, and Hoover administrations back home.

For all the seeming turpitude of their lives in the eyes of puritan America, the finest novelists of the twenties did demonstrate one over-

If the Midwest could be pastoral, it could also be stultifyingly provincial. Sherwood Anderson (above) outlined the oppressive effects of cultural sterility and conformity in Winesburg, Ohio *as did Sinclair Lewis in* Main Street. *Sauk Centre, Minnesota (below, where Lewis is shown with his first wife) served as the prototype for that novel's Gopher Prairie. Small wonder that writers like Ernest Hemingway (right) escaped to Paris.*

riding moral concern—for the highest standards of their art. Disgusted with boosterism, chauvinism, and propaganda, Hemingway would write, in *A Farewell to Arms*, that during the war:

> There were many words that you could not stand to hear and finally only the names of places had dignity. Certain numbers were the same way and certain dates and these with the names of the places were all you could say and have them mean anything. Abstract words such as glory, honor, courage, or hallow were obscene beside the concrete names of villages, the numbers of roads, the names of rivers, the numbers of regiments and the dates.

Although he began by aping the artful simplicities of Sherwood Anderson and Gertrude Stein, Hemingway found himself, like Swift in the eighteenth century and Wordsworth in the nineteenth, almost single-handedly purifying the English language of verbiage. The spare, simple prose style of *The Sun Also Rises* and the early short stories was immensely difficult to achieve, and the strain of keeping it up showed in such later novels as *For Whom the Bell Tolls* and *Across the River and Into the Trees*, with Hemingway ultimately finding it easier merely to project his own persona, a combination of daredevil warrior, bullfight *aficionado*, and big-game hunter. But when he was young and struggling to make a living while perfecting his art, he exhibited that single-minded concern for writing that was the greatest redeeming feature of so many of his dissolute contemporaries in what Gertrude Stein first called "the lost generation."

None of Hemingway's contemporaries lived a more dissolute life or wrote purer fiction than the slightly older F. Scott Fitzgerald, who did much to aid Hemingway's career in the early days in Paris. Like Hemingway, Fitzgerald led a life so flamboyant and of such symbolic significance itself that it almost, but not quite, eclipsed what really counted in it—the splendid books he managed to write under the most harrowing conditions of alcoholism, marital breakdown, and financial stress.

A remote descendant of Francis Scott Key, author of "The Star-Spangled Banner," Fitzgerald, like so many of his contemporaries, was a midwesterner come East to make his fortune. Unlike Hemingway, he was more fascinated by wealth than by death. But in his alternately lyrical and satirical examination of the world of the very rich, Fitzgerald explored all the possibilities for living the glamorous life in America and found them at best spiritually wanting, at worst destructive. He was no less sensitive to the possibilities of failure within the American system than Dreiser was, once confiding to his notebook: "I talk with the authority of failure—Ernest with the authority of success."

Fitzgerald's finest book, *The Great Gatsby*, that exquisitely wrought threnody for what Fitzgerald himself dubbed "the Jazz Age," deeply impressed Edith Wharton and struck T. S. Eliot as "the first step that American fiction has taken since Henry James." Gatsby's innocent, romantic belief in the possibilities of buying back the past is both redemptive and destructive, and he is ultimately destroyed, as was Fitzgerald, by internal weaknesses and by such "careless people" of the twenties as Gatsby's beloved Daisy Buchanan, people who "smashed up

things and creatures and then retreated back into their money. . . ."
Dying in Hollywood at forty-four, Fitzgerald never accomplished all
he meant to, but even so at least three of his five novels and a dozen of
his short stories are as fine as any in American literature.

The Great Depression of the 1930's brought home most of America's
exiled novelists, including Fitzgerald. Significantly, the greatest writer
of the period had never been abroad for long but had dug roots in his
native Mississippi soil so deep as to make his invented Yoknapatawpha
County a microcosm for life everywhere. He was William Faulkner,
whose immense output of loosely interrelated novels and stories is an
accomplishment of Balzacian magnitude, considered the greatest single
American contribution to fiction in the twentieth century.

Faulkner's imagination ranges from the highest echelons of southern society—the doomed Sartoris and Compson clans, aristocrats bled
white by the Civil War—down to the odious Snopeses, poor white
trash who proliferated in the South after the war. But vastness of scope
is not Faulkner's only accomplishment. His fellow southerner Thomas
Wolfe also attempted to capture all of America in his four mammoth
novels: *Look Homeward, Angel; Of Time and the River; The Web*

VANITY FAIR

To a world of flappers and speakeasies, of frenetic gaiety and bootleg liquor (right) F. Scott Fitzgerald gave the epigraph "the Jazz Age." He was more than a novelist and short-story writer—he was also a superb historian of America in the twenties—and the wild abandon of that era was reflected in Fitzgerald's own flamboyant lifestyle. But the flush of success and happiness manifest in the Christmas portrait of Scott, Zelda, and daughter Scotty (opposite) was ephemeral. Fitzgerald's later years were marked by alcoholism and the severe emotional and financial stress engendered by Zelda's madness.

and the Rock; and You Can't Go Home Again. Yet Wolfe's achievement now seems somehow inchoate, while Faulkner's magnificently coheres. The answer lies in Faulkner's instinctive sense of form. Wolfe, who had attended Harvard and taught English at New York University before the immense success of Look Homeward, Angel in 1929, would simply churn out vast quantities of manuscript like a man possessed. These then had to be ruthlessly cut and somehow pieced together into novels by his editors, most notably by Maxwell Perkins, who served as collaborator and midwife for Wolfe's earlier books.

Faulkner, officially uneducated and wryly proclaiming himself just a poor dirt farmer, so brilliantly absorbed the formal experiments of Joyce and other titans of modern literature and was so original himself that he was able to shape his vision of the world into structures of great beauty and power. This is especially so of his highly complex earlier works, The Sound and the Fury, As I Lay Dying, Light in August, and Absalom, Absalom! Later, like Hemingway and so many other American novelists, he seemed to get tired and tended to fall into self-imitation; what had been magnificent writing became merely mannered rhetoric, obedient to Fitzgerald's observation that "There are no second acts in American lives."

Not the least of Faulkner's accomplishments lay in showing the way to other southern writers. As late as the 1920's H. L. Mencken was able to poke cruel but hilarious fun at the inadequacies of southern culture. But with Faulkner's immense achievement, which was initially better appreciated abroad than at home, southern writers seemed emboldened to turn from lavender laments for the good old antebellum days, written in the worst genteel tradition, and to contemplate the often painful realities of their land. Writers like Robert Penn Warren, Eudora Welty, William Styron, Truman Capote, Carson McCullers, and Flannery O'Connor began writing fiction with a distinct southern accent, often dealing with Gothic horrors ultimately derived from Poe that are among the finest, if strangest, fruits of the modern American imagination. With Faulkner in the vanguard, they were able to show that the South, seemingly so cut off from the mainstream of American life after the Civil War, was in fact a unique mirror of everything grotesque and terrifying in America as a world power.

The Depression had proved a chastening experience indeed to those who had identified America with mere material grandeur, and it produced a variety of fictional responses ranging from John Steinbeck's *The Grapes of Wrath* and John Dos Passos' *U.S.A.* down to a bottomless morass of Soviet-style Socialist Realism novels that are utterly forgotten today. Although Steinbeck was always too prone to the virus of sentimentality, *The Grapes of Wrath* remains a searing indictment of the treatment of Oklahoma sharecroppers driven from their pathetic farms by the dust-bowl storms that cruelly coincided with the depths of the Depression.

Dos Passos, like Steinbeck, used a variety of documentary devices and some stream-of-consciousness effects borrowed from Joyce to give a panoramic rendition of American life in the twentieth century as seen from a basically left-wing position. In general, the Fitzgerald-Hemingway concern of the 1920's with pure art changed into a concern for social betterment, with the consequence that in a vastly different social era the novels of the 1930's have, for the most part, not worn as well as those of the earlier decade. Social concerns, however well-motivated, tend to become archaic in fiction; only art endures. What Fitzgerald once wrote about Thomas Wolfe is just as applicable to Dos Passos' magniloquent *U.S.A.* and the many other ambitious proletarian novels of the thirties:

> He has a fine inclusive mind, can write like a streak, has a great deal of emotion, though a lot of it is maudlin and inaccurate, but his awful secret transpires at every crevice—he did not have anything particular to say! The stuff about the GREAT VITAL HEART OF AMERICA is just simply corny.

Given the number of first-rate novels produced by the trauma of World War I, it was thought that World War II might be equally productive instead, it was as barren as the Civil War era as far as fiction was concerned. Some good novels did indeed appear, most notably

Norman Mailer's *The Naked and the Dead*, James Jones's *From Here to Eternity*, Irwin Shaw's *The Young Lions*, and James Gould Cozzens' *Guard of Honor*. Yet, although World War I had coincided with a worldwide flood of experimentation in all the arts, that flood had subsided by the 1940's. All that could be done to bring the novel excitingly into line with such giants of twentieth-century painting and music as Picasso and Stravinsky seemed already to have been accomplished, and there is a tame, tired quality to even the best American writing about World War II that was untrue of the novels of the earlier war.

In the postwar years, however, American fiction seemed to take on a new life, partly because of the emergence for the first time in force of new voices from minority groups. Such expert novelists as John P. Marquand, John O'Hara, James Gould Cozzens, John Updike, and Louis Auchincloss maintained a socially and aesthetically conservative tradition stemming from Henry James and Edith Wharton, but the exciting novelists of the 1950's and '60's were either southerners like William Styron and Flannery O'Connor; Jews like Saul Bellow, Bernard Malamud, and Philip Roth; or blacks like Ralph Ellison and James Baldwin. If America had not finally become democratized, it had at least found a new vitality in the fiction of its minority groups.

Because of their ethnic and social circumstances, these new novelists tended to deal with urban rather than with rural or small-town life. Saul Bellow applied the sprawling picaresque form to Chicago in *The Adventures of Augie March*, a Jewish-American descendant of Fielding's *Tom Jones*, but Bellow's finest achievement to date may be his much briefer and better controlled New York novella, *Seize the Day*, whose hapless hero wails the urban blues. Similarly, the hero of Ralph Ellison's highly innovative *Invisible Man* comes north to New York to experience the terrifying invisibility of a black man in a white culture.

The new insights into American life provided by the minority novelists are perceptive and exciting but may not reach real fruition because of the competing claims of journalism, the movies, and television for writers' and readers' attention. The most obvious effect of this —and the most dangerous for the future of American fiction—is the way in which so many novelists have turned to the far more profitable medium of nonfiction. Truman Capote calling his splendid account of a brutal midwestern killing, *In Cold Blood*, a "nonfiction novel" is but one ominous symptom of this trend. In the heyday of the novel such a documentary account of an actual murder might have provided the impetus for *The Red and the Black*, *Crime and Punishment*, or *An American Tragedy*. The decline of the novel in the present day no doubt helped determine Capote to convert his fine fictional talent to the writing of nonfiction.

Similarly, Ralph Ellison has been silent for many years and Norman Mailer has spent far more time and earned far more money writing imaginative journalism than fiction. One of the most outstanding accomplishments of the new American novelists has been their skill in merging fact with fiction, but it is a dubious accomplishment as far as the art of the novel is concerned when it entails a far less happy merging of art with the marketplace.

The southern literary tradition found its most profound exponent in William Faulkner (above, left). Another southerner whose scope was as vast was Thomas Wolfe (above, right), whose epic first novel, Look Homeward, Angel, *was published on the eve of the Great Depression. The economic desperation of the thirties fueled a large body of proletarian fiction, none finer than* The Grapes of Wrath *by John Steinbeck (opposite). His subject was the sharecroppers who were forced to abandon the drought-stricken farms of the Southwest (below).*

7

Era of Experimentation

JUST AS THE PUBLICATION of *Sister Carrie* in 1900 may be said to herald the birth of the modern American novel, so may we date the twentieth-century British novel from the publication in that same year of Joseph Conrad's masterpiece, *Lord Jim.* In the preface to *The Nigger of the 'Narcissus,'* written two years earlier, Conrad had set forth his credo in these ringing terms: "A work that aspires, however humbly, to the condition of art should carry its justification in every line." At least as far as he was concerned, the good old Victorian days of the ramshackle three-decker serialized novel filled with padding, slapdash improvisation, and penny-dreadful plotting were over.

One of the minor ironies of British literary history is that the man who brought high artistic conscience to the modern novel was not an Englishman at all but a Pole. Conrad's real name was Teodor Jósef Konrad Korzeniowski, and he first glimpsed England in 1878, the year he joined the British merchant service.

The son of a Polish writer and translator who was exiled to Russia for his participation in Polish revolutionary groups, Conrad spent the first half of his career as a sailor. For a time he seemed destined to roam the world as an eternal exile, spending many years aboard English merchant ships, mostly in the South Pacific, the Indian Ocean, the Malayan archipelago, and the Belgian Congo. When he began writing fiction, while still a sailor, Conrad had the unique problem of choosing which language to function in, a problem he solved—or so he later claimed—by writing in English, thinking in French, and dreaming in Polish.

With the publication of The Nigger of the 'Narcissus,' Lord Jim, Youth, *and* Typhoon, *Joseph Conrad became typed as a masterful spinner of sea yarns. Today, however, the Polish-born English writer is recognized for bringing a high artistic conscience and a sophisticated narrative technique to the novel.*

Elsewhere in the preface to *The Nigger of the 'Narcissus'* Conrad avers: "My task, which I am trying to achieve is, by the power of the written word to make you hear, to make you feel—it is, above all, to make you *see*. That—and no more, and it is everything." And with the highest Flaubertian ideals of fiction, Conrad did indeed make us see the exotic Eastern world in a series of novels and stories impressive both in their variety and their profundity of vision. Because of such early sea stories as *The Nigger, Lord Jim, Youth*, and *Typhoon*, Conrad became typed in the public mind as a masterful spinner of sea yarns and a Kiplingesque prophet of empire. He resented this glib identification, and in the masterpieces of his middle years—*Nostromo, The Secret Agent*, and *Under Western Eyes*—he turned almost entirely from the sea to the world of politics and revolution. Thus *The Secret Agent* is land-

Like Conrad (far left), H. G. Wells (left) had many careers; in addition to being an author, he was a scientist, an educator, and a social prophet. He wrote some of the finest science fiction that genre has ever known, but he also produced social comedies and works that were frankly propagandistic. He was immensely popular in his own time, as was his friend, novelist Arnold Bennett (below, right). The third member of the triumvirate that dominated Edwardian fiction was John Galsworthy (below). His work satirized Britain's upper classes, most notably in The Forsyte Saga.

locked in London, *Under Western Eyes* is set in Russia and Switzerland, and *Nostromo* is a deeply imagined history and geography of a Latin American country in the throes of revolution.

What Conrad's early audiences generally failed to grasp was that he was no writer of boys' adventure stories in the tradition of Cooper or Captain Marryat but a highly complex artist and moralist, one who used the sea as a symbol for man's alienation in a hostile universe. This implied, in Conrad's mind, the necessity of steadfastness and solidarity if the human community—so well symbolized by a ship precariously afloat in dangerous waters—were to survive. To this task Conrad brought a gorgeous English prose style and a sophisticated narrative technique involving time shifts and, more often than not, a series of stories-within-stories, usually presided over by his favorite narrator, the wise old salt Marlow, who is as aware as Conrad is of the capacity for betrayal and moral darkness in the human heart, "the true horror behind the appalling face of things" that this most pessimistic of novelists saw through his Slavic eyes.

As thoroughly English in sensibility as Conrad was piquantly foreign, Herbert George Wells resembled his contemporary and friend in having had more than one career. Wells, indeed, managed to combine in his long lifetime the roles of scientist, social prophet, educator of the masses, ladies' man, and prolific author of more than one hundred books that fall into three general categories. First there are the "scientific romances" he began writing in the 1890's, books that won him immediate popularity. Such novels as *The Time Machine* and *The War of the Worlds* are not merely prophetic, they use the science-fiction form to make political and social statements as well. Thus they are much more thoughtful than the otherwise similar novels of Jules Verne, Wells's only real competitor in the early days of the genre.

Then come a series of social comedies about contemporary English lower-middle-class life, written in a somewhat Dickensian, breezily humorous style. These novels usually deal with a hero who attempts to escape his stifling position in society to live a richer, more exciting life than that offered generally to shop assistants by the late Victorian and Edwardian worlds. *Love and Mr. Lewisham, Kipps,* and *The History of Mr. Polly* are characteristic of this side of Wells, but the most triumphant novel of this sort is *Tono-Bungay,* a hilarious dissection of the business ethic that had come to dominate twentieth-century life and that is employed in the novel to foist on a gullible public the totally worthless patent medicine of the title.

Finally, there are the less successful novels of Wells's later career, books in which a thin veneer of fiction is used to sugarcoat the various social and political dogmas Wells propounded. Never as interested in the pure art of the novel as his friends and contemporaries James, Conrad, and Stephen Crane were, Wells allowed his fictional technique to degenerate while his prophetic voice became ever more strident—with the effect of rendering his later novels almost unreadable. Wells, who was born the year after the American Civil War ended and who died the year World War II ended, lived long enough to see all his hopeful plans for the reconstruction of human society along scientific and rational lines come to grief in the mad holocaust of total war, and he died a disillusioned, heartbroken man.

As popular as Wells, and nearly as prolific, was his friend Arnold Bennett, who, with Wells and Galsworthy—all three of whom were born within a year of each other—dominated the Edwardian literary scene. Bennett was more interested in the art of fiction, however, and less interested in science and politics than was Wells. He was determined to do for his native Staffordshire, and especially the so-called "Five Towns" of the pottery district there, what such French realists as Flaubert, Maupassant, and Zola had done for their native regions. He also determined to apply their objective techniques to the rendering of English life, but his own ebullient good humor often interfered with his theoretical devotion to grim realism, producing in his masterpiece, *The Old Wives' Tale,* a novel less aesthetically rigorous but much livelier than those of the French realists and such British disciples as George Gissing and George Moore.

In *The Old Wives' Tale* Bennett was consciously improving on Maupassant's novel, *A Woman's Life.* Instead of one heroine, his work has two, the Baines sisters of Bursley (one of the Five Towns), who live very different lives in their youth but who end their days together with the same stoical fortitude Bennett saw as characteristic of his native region. Because of his immense popularity and his insatiable desire for high living (he once vowed he would write himself a yacht —and did), Bennett was tempted to overproduce, with the result that too much of his writing is hackwork. But he was never less than hugely entertaining, and in his fine autobiographical Clayhanger trilogy he once again touched the fictional heights he had achieved in *The Old Wives' Tale.*

Both Bennett and Wells came from the very lowest rungs of the lower middle class. In sharp contrast, the third member of the great Edwardian triumvirate, John Galsworthy, was a rich patrician trained in the law who didn't have to write for a living but who nevertheless produced novels and plays that were great popular successes. He is best remembered today for the *The Forsyte Saga*, a nine-novel epic of upper-middle-class life that spans half a century (from the 1880's to the 1930's) and begins with *The Man of Property*, his finest single achievement. The subsequent eight novels in the *Saga* are weaker, showing Galsworthy's besetting sins of sentimentality and glibness. But *The Man of Property* still retains its force, largely because it was based on an unhappy episode in Galsworthy's otherwise placid life, one that began when he found himself in love with his cousin's wife and had to wait for nine frustrating years until she was able to obtain a divorce and marry him. The love triangle of Soames and Irene Forsyte and the young architect Philip Bosinney derives directly from Galsworthy's own life, and it is treated with a combination of ironic wit and emotional fervor that diminishes in his later fiction. *The Man of Property* is not only a deeply felt love story but a brilliant anatomization of the materialism and snobbery of the late Victorian upper class that Galsworthy knew so well and felt so ambivalent about.

Despite, or perhaps because of, their vast popularity with the reading public, the great Edwardian novelists came under fierce attack from the generation that matured in the years just before World War I and particularly from one of its most eloquent spokesmen, Virginia Woolf, who announced in a 1924 Cambridge lecture that "in or about December, 1910, human character changed." It wasn't human nature that had changed, of course, but rather the novelist's way of perceiving and rendering it. To Virginia Woolf and her more serious contemporaries, the shared literary method of Wells, Bennett, and Galsworthy, which involved a saturation in material fact and a chronological ordering of events, was inadequate to capture the evanescent shimmerings of a sensitively apprehended reality. Decrying what she saw as the Edwardians' ponderous materialism, Virginia Woolf insisted that "Life is not a series of gig lamps symmetrically arranged; but a luminous halo, a semi-transparent envelope surrounding us from the beginning of consciousness to the end," and that it is the novelist's duty to capture that halo on paper much as the French Impressionist painters had captured light on canvas —to "record the atoms as they fell upon the mind in the order in which they fall," rather than in a neat but unrealistic chronology.

And so the battle was joined. The Edwardian novelists were too successful by this time to care much about replying to Virginia Woolf or to the novelists of her generation on whose behalf she was arguing. Yet so striking is the difference between the Edwardian and the Georgian concepts of fiction that it does indeed seem as if human nature itself had changed between the death of Edward VII and the coronation of George V in 1910. Who was this strange, ethereal woman who helped bring about such a revolution in fiction, this woman whose awesome powers as a novelist inspired the nervously mocking title of Edward Albee's play, *Who's Afraid of Virginia Woolf?* She was, before all else, the daughter of Sir Leslie Stephen, one of the most prestigious Victorian men of letters and editor of *The Dictionary of National Biography*, whose first wife (who was not Virginia's mother) was Thackeray's daughter. Hence Virginia grew up in a highly literate household, and on the death of her father in 1904 she settled with her

sister Vanessa—herself a talented artist—in the Bloomsbury section of London, where the two Stephen girls became the nucleus for a clan of artists and intellectuals later known as the Bloomsbury Group. These distinguished young people, most of them Cambridge graduates, included, at one time or another, the novelist E. M. Forster, the biographer Lytton Strachey, the art critic Clive Bell (who later married Vanessa), the poet T. S. Eliot, the economist John Maynard Keynes, and the journalist, civil servant, and liberal propagandist Leonard Woolf, who married Virginia in 1912 and spent the years until her suicide in 1941 tenderly looking after her.

Her willed end came as no particular surprise to those who knew Virginia Woolf, for she had always been extremely high-strung and at several points in her life had suffered complete nervous breakdowns brought on by overwork. Partly as occupational therapy, Leonard and Virginia began printing and publishing books on a hand press they called the Hogarth Press, still in existence today. Her own career as a novelist began with two fine but relatively conventional books, *The Voyage Out* and *Night and Day*. It wasn't until she wrote *Jacob's Room* in 1922 that her real experimentation in the novel began, and these experiments culminated in her greatest achievements, *Mrs. Dalloway*, *To the Lighthouse*, and *The Waves*. Largely discarding the received conventions of the realistic English novel as practiced by Bennett, Galsworthy, and Wells, Virginia Woolf played all sorts of tricks with time, with limited point of view, and with what later generations would come to call "stream of consciousness." Her highly sophisticated sense of reality called for an almost entirely different aesthetic of the novel from that of her predecessors, and in both her voluminous diaries and her articles for the *Times Literary Supplement* she eloquently defended her techniques and those of such contemporaries as Joyce and Lawrence (though she had little else in common with either man).

Mrs. Dalloway, like Joyce's *Ulysses*, is confined to the thoughts and actions of a single day. We see London through the eyes of Clarissa Dalloway, wife of a distinguished but rather distant member of Parliament, as she goes about her errands for a party she is giving that night. Counterpointed against her vision is the vision of Septimus Warren Smith, a young shell-shocked war veteran whose path occasionally crosses Mrs. Dalloway's, neither knowing of the other's existence. With subtly integrated flashbacks we get to know much about the past of Clarissa Dalloway and her friends. At the same time we get an even stronger sense of the loneliness of the individual consciousness in a great city, the ineffectual reaching out for human solidarity, the moments of sensual bliss and metaphysical despair that come to all of us but which only Virginia Woolf seems sensitive enough to capture and vividly render. There is every reason for novelists to be afraid of Virginia Woolf, born with the thinnest of skins but with a prodigious talent for fiction. The rest of us can only rejoice in the heightened sensitivity to life she can give us.

On the surface, the achievement of James Joyce seems similar, but actually, as Virginia Woolf keenly realized, their differences of temperament and upbringing sharply divided them. Joyce was an exact con-

Like Virginia Woolf, James Joyce (left) was more concerned with inner experience than with external reality. These two inaugurators of the twentieth-century novel were exact contemporaries but led very different existences. Virginia Woolf lived and worked in the center of the English literary establishment; Joyce wrote his novels in self-imposed exile on the Continent. The odyssey depicted in Joyce's Ulysses is a journey into the consciousnesses of the novel's three main characters as well as being a journey through Dublin (below). Because of its alleged obscenity, Ulysses was long banned in the English-speaking world. The problem of censorship also beset D. H. Lawrence (right), whose Lady Chatterley's Lover, written in 1928, was banned in the United States until 1959.

temporary of Virginia Woolf, but while Woolf lived all her life in the center of the English literary establishment, Joyce, born into a seedy lower-middle-class family in Dublin, spent his mature life in self-imposed exile in Trieste, Zurich, and Paris, where he engaged in a lifelong struggle for artistic integrity against the forces of poverty, blindness, and censorship. Educated by Jesuits, he fled the narrow provincialism of Ireland to become an English teacher at the Berlitz school in Trieste, where his phenomenal command of languages helped, but his failing eyesight hindered, his making any sort of conventional living.

His first volume, a collection of related short stories called *Dubliners*, achieved publication only after a death struggle against censorship, something Joyce was to be dogged by throughout his career. The stories in *Dubliners* are relatively conventional in form, although like Chekhov's they rely more on mood and atmosphere than on plotting.

The climax of each story is what Joyce called an "epiphany"—a sudden revelation to the central character of what his life has been all about, revelations so subtle that they quite elude the careless reader. From the entire volume emerges a sense of Dublin as a gray, depressing city whose frustrated inhabitants go about sodden with rain, beer, and self-pity. Joyce's rendering of all this is itself pitiless, however; he is as far as it is possible to be from such gregarious, self-projecting novelists as Thackeray who take their readers in hand and explain just what can be gotten out of their stories.

In 1914 Joyce's first novel, *A Portrait of the Artist as a Young Man*, was published. In its hero, Stephen Dedalus, Joyce had indeed portrayed himself—proud, intellectual, austere—and his revolt against the restrictions of his sordid family life. All the events of the novel are seen through Stephen's eyes and are filtered through his increasingly complex mind. Thus the first line of the novel is almost baby talk: "Once upon a time and a very good time it was there was a moocow coming down along the road and this moocow that was coming down the road met a nicens little boy named baby tuckoo. . . ." But by the end of the novel we are treated to a whole dissertation on St. Thomas Aquinas. Between babyhood and young adulthood have come a variety of autobiographical experiences in which Stephen painfully develops his own intellect and consciousness against the garrulous shallowness of his father, the religious bigotry of the rest of his family, the bombastic nationalism of his schoolmates, and the provincialism of Ireland.

In a sense, Joyce's masterpiece, *Ulysses*, is a sequel to *Portrait*. Once again Stephen Dedalus is a major figure, but in this vastly larger and richer novel he is joined by Leopold and Molly Bloom, other centers of consciousness. Stephen, still the lonely, arrogant would-be artist, is counterpointed against Leopold Bloom—who, as a Jew in Dublin, is similarly isolated—and against his even more sensual wife, Molly, who in the course of the single day of the novel's events, June 16, 1904, betrays her husband. By the end of the day Stephen has made fortuitous contact with the Blooms and is essentially adopted by them, finding the father he feels he never really had in Leopold and an earth mother's warmth in Molly.

To tell the story not only of Stephen and the Blooms but of all life in Dublin on one specific day, Joyce employed a variety of techniques that still astound in their virtuosity and inventiveness. On one level, for instance, *Ulysses* is a reworking in modern terms of Homer's epic with specific, if often highly recondite, references to the *Odyssey*: Bloom is Odysseus; Stephen, his son Telemachus; Molly, his not entirely virtuous helpmeet, Penelope. Cyclops appears as a bigoted Irishman in a pub, Nausicaa as a lovely girl glimpsed on a beach.

Throughout the novel we see all events exclusively through the minds of either Stephen, Leopold, or Molly, with absolutely no helpful intervention on Joyce's part. In a sense he is searching for an ultimate realism of presentation, forcing the reader to use his imagination throughout to understand what, at any given moment, has prompted the variegated shifts in the characters' streams of consciousness. Thus enlisting the readers' empathetic cooperation, Joyce made the reading of *Ulysses* a difficult but bracing task, one aided by a gusty, often ribald humor missing from the generally dour pages of *Portrait*.

Partly because of the scandals associated with the publication of *Ulysses*, long banned in the English-speaking world for its alleged obscenity, it became the most notorious novel of the twentieth century. From the start, however, more serious readers clearly realized that it was also perhaps the most significant novel ever written; that it both summed up the concerns and techniques of all previous fiction and formed a dead end for future novelists. It was almost a dead end for Joyce, too, for in his last novel, *Finnegans Wake*, he found himself pushed into rendering the dream world of a single, archetypal character in the course of one night's sleep.

Because of the distortions of dreams, *Finnegans Wake* is even more difficult to follow than *Ulysses*, which deals at least with the relatively coherent daylight world. In rendering the troubled night of his hero, H. C. Earwicker (alias Here Comes Everybody), Joyce tried to embody symbolically every myth known to man; to allude, through infinitely complex multilingual puns, to every known language; to sum up nothing less than man's entire experience on earth. This highly ambitious plan succeeds for some readers, who regard *Finnegans Wake* as not only the ultimate novel but the Ultimate Wisdom; other readers, put off by the almost impenetrable language, fail to see it as a novel at all but as a giant, pedantic practical joke. The truth no doubt lies somewhere in between, but problematical though the place of *Finnegans Wake* is in world fiction, there is no gainsaying the immense influence Joyce's whole career has exerted on novelists to the present day.

One stumbling block in appreciating Joyce during his lifetime was his alleged obsession with sex, although to us he seems only to have been interested in giving sex a role in the novel equivalent to its importance in real life. Equally plagued during his lifetime by the stupidly censorious was the third titan of the modern British novel, David Herbert Lawrence. The son of a Nottingham coal miner, Lawrence as a boy witnessed the struggle between his crudely vital father and his genteel, possessive mother for dominance in the family, a struggle that went into the making of Lawrence's great novel, the highly autobiographical *Sons and Lovers*, which was published in 1913, just before Joyce's analagously autobiographical *Portrait of the Artist*. The year before, Lawrence had met Frieda von Richthofen, sister of the famous German air ace of World War I and wife of an English professor. Lawrence and Frieda ran off together, marrying in 1914, and after the war they traveled widely in Europe and America, living at various times in Italy, New Mexico, and Mexico as the tubercular Lawrence relentlessly sought better health in sunnier climes.

Meanwhile, Lawrence wrote two related novels, *The Rainbow* and *Women in Love*, in which he explored, with a profundity and moral seriousness rarely encountered in previous British fiction, the true meaning of the relations between the sexes. Both books were condemned as "dirty" when they appeared; *The Rainbow* was suppressed shortly after its publication in 1915. Yet today both novels seem lyrical and tender in their evocations of love and psychologically acute in their

James Joyce's staunchest champion in his battle against censorship was Sylvia Beach. The visionary owner of the Paris bookstore Shakespeare and Company recognized Ulysses *as a masterpiece and published it in 1922. The United States ban against the book was not lifted until eleven years later.*

analysis of the conflicting love demands of the sexes. If Lawrence didn't quite stand the novel on its head as Joyce had, he did make a major contribution in giving the novel new materials to work with. And, as fine a poet as he was a novelist, Lawrence wrote a highly individual prose style rich in symbolism and imagery.

The older and sicker Lawrence became, however, the more shrill and didactic his tone was to grow, so that such late novels as *The Plumed Serpent* and *Lady Chatterley's Lover* resemble not so much novels as impassioned sermons on the proper relations of the sexes in a modern world devoid of religion, myth, and ritual and given over to a materialistic use of sex abhorrent to the profoundly puritanical, rather humorless Lawrence.

One of Lawrence's major disciples was the brilliantly humorous Aldous Huxley, who, with Evelyn Waugh, brought to the English novel between the world wars a satiric verve almost wholly lacking in Lawrence's rather portentous sermonizing. Like all major satirists, however, neither Huxley nor Waugh could sustain for long the utterly nihilistic visions of the modern world so wittily captured in Huxley's *Antic Hay* and *Point Counter Point* or Waugh's *Decline and Fall* and *Vile Bodies*. Huxley ultimately retreated into a personal mysticism derived partly from Eastern religions and partly from the use of such consciousness-expanding drugs as mescaline; Waugh took the more conventional route of Catholicism, but in both cases the quest for religious affirmation put an end to the satiric visions of their youth.

With such giants as Woolf, Joyce, and Lawrence hovering over it, the British novel has had difficulty finding viable new directions to take since the 1940s, but as one of the most literate nations on earth Britain has had no lack of superb talents writing fiction. Both in his lighter works and his more serious novels, Graham Greene, for instance, has brought a high degree of skill to the thriller, seeing in it a paradigm for the pursuit of God by man and the conflict between good and evil in the human soul, and rendering the seedier aspects of modern urban life with a precision and sympathy far more poetic than anything achieved by earlier, naturalistic novelists.

Anthony Powell, in his ambitious series *A Dance to the Music of Time*, has combined a Proustian sense of the past with the kind of social satire practiced by Waugh, but he is neither as profound as the former nor as fiercely witty as the latter. Lawrence Durrell, in his *Alexandria Quartet*, reverts to the exoticism of Conrad as well as the moral relativism of Proust; and C. P. Snow, in his *Strangers and Brothers* cycle, to the placidly intelligent but uninnovative realism of Trollope. For a while after World War II such "angry young men" as Kingsley Amis and John Wain brought back the earthy, lower-middle-class comedy of Wells and Bennett to the contemporary English social situation, and such highly talented women novelists as Doris Lessing, Iris Murdoch, and Muriel Spark have shown that a tradition of perceptive women novelists going back to Fanny Burney and Jane Austen is still alive and well in England. But no single figure dominates the current English fictional scene as impressively as Joyce, Lawrence, and Woolf did half a century ago.

8

Daydreams and Nightmares

IN GERMANY, AS IN RUSSIA, the novel came relatively late on the literary scene, emerging not so much from the rise of the middle class in the eighteenth century as from the romantic revolution of the early nineteenth century. Indeed, romanticism was practically a German invention, taking earlier and stronger hold there than anywhere else in Europe or in America. With its natural offspring, nationalism, it has dominated German thought and letters ever since.

An awareness of the dual nature of man—part earthbound, part soaring through a dream world of concocted fancy and imagination—has been a characteristic of all great German novelists since Goethe's day, a list that includes the classicists of the Enlightenment and the romantics of the nineteenth century as well as such twentieth-century novelists as Herman Hesse and Ernst Jünger. It has also dictated the two forms that German fiction has found especially congenial: the *Bildungsroman*, the loosely autobiographical novel; and the fantasy, which sometimes takes the form of philosophical allegory or psychological horror story.

Bildungsroman is practically an untranslatable word, which is why it has been retained in other languages as the term for a certain kind of novel. Essentially, the *Bildungsroman* is concerned with the development of its hero's mind and personality through a series of significant encounters with the world that bring him to terms with the society surrounding him. Characteristically, it focuses on the years of adolescence and young adulthood; on the hero's struggle for independence from his parents and the stifling, bourgeois world they inhabit; on his first love, usually unrequited; on his rejection of conventional learning and his search for meaningful expression of his personality through art; and on his emergence, battle-scarred but victorious, as a whole being functioning in the social world, his personal egoism repressed or sublimated to the extent that he can find a place among his fellow beings.

Other nations besides Germany have produced *Bildungsromane* of great distinction. One thinks of the Frenchman Romain Rolland and *Jean-Christophe*, his massive epic of the development of a great composer, a life loosely modeled on Beethoven's. The British novel has been rich in *Bildungsromane*, ranging from Dickens's *David Copperfield* and Meredith's *The Ordeal of Richard Feverel* in the 1850's to Lawrence's *Sons and Lovers*, Joyce's *A Portrait of the Artist*, and Maugham's *Of Human Bondage* in the early twentieth century. And the British have not neglected the novel of woman's development either, as witness Charlotte Brontë's *Jane Eyre* and Dorothy Richardson's immense *Pilgrimage* series. But nowhere has the form been so crucial to the art of fiction as in Germany, starting with the *Wilhelm Meister* of the protean Johann Wolfgang von Goethe, and reaching its apogee in Thomas Mann's *The Magic Mountain*.

Although one thinks of Goethe primarily as a poet and dramatist, his contributions to the German novel are of such significance that he makes an ideal starting point. For Goethe, like Pushkin, applied his poetic gifts to the creation of a distinctive national fiction. Born in 1749, Goethe began his long literary career as a lyric poet and romantic dramatist. But his frustrated love for Charlotte Buff while he was a young law student in Wetzlar led to the writing of his first novel, *The Sorrows of Young Werther*, in 1774. Like so much eighteenth-century fiction, *Werther* was narrated by means of letters, but it brought to that already sagging form a romantic intensity so revolutionary in spirit that this brief novel, which reads so absurdly today, enthralled Europe and made Goethe world-famous practically overnight, much as *Childe Harold* was later to do for Lord Byron, a fellow romantic whom Goethe much admired.

The impact of *Werther* caused many an unrequited lover to emulate its self-pitying, alienated hero by committing suicide, and, in a sense, *Werther* was as influential on the attitudes and life-styles of romantic European youth as *Uncle Tom's Cabin* would be on the climate of opinion that led to the American Civil War. In both cases the novel's impact was disproportionate to its purely aesthetic qualities, and in the case of *Werther* the shock waves it sent forth had not fully subsided even by 1939, when Thomas Mann paid it ironic tribute in *Lotte in Weimar*, his tale of the aged Goethe's meeting with his Charlotte.

Despite the characteristically romantic *Sturm und Drang*, or "storm and stress," of *Werther*, Goethe himself was preeminently a survivor. Far from committing suicide, he went on to become a jurist, critic, scientist, painter, theatrical manager, governmental administrator, and, above all, the olympian poet-dramatist of *Faust*. As he grew older his romantic ardor cooled; he found new virtues in the once-despised classicism, and he managed, ultimately, to fuse classic form with romantic passion much as his friend Beethoven did in music.

This later spirit reached fruition in the great *Bildungsroman* entitled *Wilhelm Meister*, which Goethe began writing as early as the 1770's but did not complete until 1829, three years before his death. In tracing Wilhelm's education in life, especially through his experiences in a small wandering troupe of theater people, Goethe relied heavily on his own experiences. It is unfortunate that *Wilhelm Meister* is known to English readers only in the rather stodgy and obscure translation of Thomas Carlyle, for, almost unique in the annals of autobiographical fiction, it is notably lacking in self-pity, the endemic curse of the genre.

The other dominant German fictional preoccupation—fantasy—was developed not by Goethe but by his fellow romantics, E.T.A. Hoffmann and Heinrich von Kleist. Hoffmann is known to non-German readers chiefly through Offenbach's opera, *The Tales of*

The Sorrows of Young Werther established Johann von Goethe as Germany's quintessential romantic in much the same way that Childe Harold's Pilgrimage *would later confirm Lord Byron's similar position in England. Goethe was to explore many different aspects of romanticism (two illustrations from his diverse works are shown at right), and in his later years he was even to come to terms with the classicism he had so vehemently rejected in his youth. In the writings of E.T.A. Hoffman (above) another important element of German romanticism— fantasy—was introduced.*

Hoffmann, but charming as that work is it no more does justice to a remarkable writer than Ambroise Thomas's *Mignon* does to *Wilhelm Meister* or Gounod's *Faust* does to Goethe's supreme achievement. To some extent Hoffmann deserved, and might even have applauded, Offenbach's opera, for he himself was a skilled composer and an influential operatic producer. But Hoffmann's real fame is based on his tales of fantasy and the grotesque, usually centering on the bizarre adventures of his autobiographical hero, the musician Johannes Kreisler, whose eccentricities inspired Robert Schumann's set of piano pieces, *Kreisleriana*. To English-speaking readers, Hoffmann's tales seem reminiscent of Poe, but the German's fantasies are less personally paranoid than the American's and are usually more humorous, whimsical, and allegorical in nature. Romantic idealism and the desire to escape from the daily grind of humdrum duty into a world of the imagination, so fruitful in German art and so destructive in German politics, are all to be found in Hoffmann's haunted—and haunting—tales, and they find even more profound psychological expression in the horror-saturated stories of Heinrich von Kleist, whose suicide at thirty-five robbed German literature of one of its most original figures.

Given this penchant for almost hysterical romanticism, it is hardly surprising that the German novel had little to contribute to the late-nineteenth-century development of solid, mundane realism. There is no German equivalent of a Flaubert, a George Eliot, or a Tolstoy, and as a result such German realists as Jeremias Gotthelf and Theodor Fontane seem somewhat provincial figures, of almost purely local interest, especially when compared to the giants of European realism. This generalization is particularly unfair to Fontane, whose *Before the Storm*, about Prussian life during the Napoleonic Wars, is perhaps the greatest of German historical novels and not unworthy to stand beside Manzoni's *The Betrothed*, if not Stendhal's *Charterhouse of Parma*, in that genre. More particularly relevant today are Fontane's sympathetic novels about the condition of women in the nineteenth century, among which *Effi Briest* is especially outstanding. Effi, in her search for fulfillment outside the bonds of marriage and the general restrictions imposed on women, is a German sister to Flaubert's Emma Bovary, Ibsen's Nora Helmer, and Kate Chopin's Edna Pontellier, the dissatisfied heroine of that remarkably prophetic American novel, *The Awakening*, published in 1899—four years after *Effi Briest*.

Despite these isolated successes, however, the German novel did not begin to impinge seriously and steadily on world literature until the twentieth century—partly, perhaps, because Germany herself came so late to a consciousness of national identity. Like Italy, Germany attained full political unification only in the last half of the nineteenth century, and in both countries the development of the novel lagged accordingly. But in the twentieth century Germany—or at least German-speaking writers—had an enormous impact on the novel. There is nothing provincial about such modern masters as Mann, Kafka, Musil, or Hesse; indeed, they themselves have exerted a major influence on world literature while continuing to work in the traditional, idiomatically German forms of the *Bildungsroman* and the fantasy.

Mann in particular enjoyed a world reputation—ratified by his winning the Nobel Prize for literature in 1929—as the spokesman, both in his personal life and in his art, for all that was valuable in the German tradition. Yet like Goethe he was more concerned with being a good European than merely a good German. He came by his cosmopolitan outlook naturally, for while his father was a solidly respectable Lübeck businessman, his mother was of Creole and Brazilian descent. Mann always keenly felt the mixture in his blood of North and South, attributing to his paternal ancestry his puritan devotion to hard work, to his mother's influence his sensual apprehension of life and art. Much of his fiction is therefore devoted to conflicts between the German and the Mediterranean, between the bohemian and the bourgeois, between physical and moral health and disease. In his masterpiece, *The Magic Mountain*, an Alpine tuberculosis sanatorium becomes a microcosm for all Europe, and Hans Castorp, the callow hero—"life's delicate child" as Mann semi-ironically dubs him—learns, in true *Bildungsroman* fashion, all that Western culture has to teach during the seven years he stays there. Ironically, he is cured of both his tuberculosis and his naïveté just in time to become a soldier in World War I.

Thus *The Magic Mountain* becomes a vastly ambitious summa of European culture in the last days before its dissolution. Much later, in *Doctor Faustus*, Mann would treat the same theme after the even greater holocaust of World War II, blending in incomparable fashion the Faust legend with the Nazi takeover of Germany as experienced

Johann von Goethe was a poet, a novelist, and a dramatist. His output was prodigious, and his influence, through works like Wilhelm Meister, *was enormous. The latter, a Bildungsroman or novel of personal development, was an excellent early example of what was to prove Germany's most enduring literary genre. Late in life Goethe spent several years in Italy (above), gaining inspiration for the verse-dramas* Iphigenia in Tauris, Egmont, *and* Torquato Tasso.

by one of his most fascinating artist figures, the demon-possessed composer Adrian Leverkühn.

Mann's sense of the artist as an equivocal if not downright dangerous figure outside society permeates all his fiction in varied guises. In the giant tetralogy, *Joseph and His Brothers*, which occupied him throughout the 1930's, the biblical Joseph becomes an artist-hero whose social innovations are based on President Roosevelt's New Deal. In one of the finest novellas ever written, *Death in Venice*, the artist is a writer whose lifelong austerity and devotion to his craft break down in the "dangerous" southern atmosphere of corrupt Venice, where he falls hopelessly in love with a beautiful boy who represents the typical Mann triad of beauty, the erotic, and death. The artist appears for the last time in *The Confessions of Felix Krull*, this time as a trickster whose pranks enliven the most comic of Mann's great novels.

Although Mann had generally supported the German position in World War I, he was so eloquently anti-Nazi that he had to flee Germany in 1933, living first in Switzerland and ultimately, throughout the war years, in Pacific Palisades, California, where he was part of a colony of distinguished German émigrés that included the composer Arnold Schoenberg, the conductor Bruno Walter, and the novelist Franz Werfel. In lectures, pamphlets, and radio broadcasts, he inveighed against the Nazi regime, hoping to rally the ever-diminishing, saving remnant of the Germany he had grown up in.

Mann's older brother, Heinrich, was also a skilled novelist and author of *The Blue Angel*, source of a brilliant motion picture. But Thomas Mann's position among German writers was unique, and despite the occasional density and pedantry of his style, he found a worldwide audience from the time of his first novel, *Buddenbrooks*, written when he was only twenty-five, until his death in 1955 at the age of eighty.

Quite the opposite was the case of Mann's great contemporary Franz Kafka. His three novels went unpublished during his lifetime and he ordered his friend and biographer, Max Brod, to destroy them after his death. Brod wisely ignored this wish, and as consequence we have *The Trial*, *The Castle*, and *Amerika*, three of the strangest and most haunting novels of our time. Some thirty years after Kafka's death in 1924, W. H. Auden said: "Had one to name the author who comes nearest to bearing the same kind of relation to our age as Dante, Shakespeare and Goethe bore to theirs, Kafka is the first one would think of."

Born into a well-to-do German-speaking Jewish family in Prague, Kafka spent his brief, father-dominated, and tuberculosis-ridden life as a clerk in an insurance office. He never married, although he was engaged on two separate occasions. He published very little, and that mostly in Yiddish newspapers. Intensely neurotic and self-doubting, Kafka probably lacked the assurance and equanimity necessary to produce long fiction, and in fact his novels—great though they are—are essentially fragmentary; his best and most characteristic work came in shorter forms, either as stories, quasi-Talmudic parables, or even as one-line epigrams and notebook entries.

In the feverish intensity of his stories, Kafka seems the heir to Kleist, whom he much admired, and to the general German tradition of the macabre fantasy. One of the greatest of his stories, *Metamorphosis*, begins thus: "As Gregor Samsa awoke one morning from uneasy dreams he found himself transformed in his bed into a gigantic insect." For the next sixty-odd pages we experience bourgeois life from the point of view of a grotesque, giant cockroach.

Where Kafka differs from most earlier writers of fantasy, though, is in the ironic humor he brings to bear on his tales of terror and in their haunting, often prophetic, allegorical quality. Although Kafka died a decade before the Nazis came to power he seemed to foresee the horrors that awaited mankind. It is part of his prophetic genius that in a story like *The Penal Colony* he could envision the way in which modern methods of mass production would be utilized for mass destruction. And in *The Trial*, his autobiographical, rather Chaplinesque hero, "K," is tried for a mysterious crime he has not even heard about, much in the manner of the Soviet purge trials of the 1930's.

A deep, Kierkegaardian "fear and trembling" about God, a metaphysical angst, underlies all of Kafka's stories, so that however brief some of them are, and however pellucid their surface—and Kafka did write some of the clearest German prose of any novelist—each of them exists on many levels of meaning. Although he was essentially a miniaturist in spirit, his works most closely resemble the gigantic symphonies of a fellow German-Jewish Czech, Gustav Mahler. These are equally permeated with a sense of terror and impending doom mingled with wry, sardonic wit and concern for the destiny of suffering humanity.

Another Czech whom Kafka resembles is the writer Jaroslav Hasek, whose masterpiece, *The Good Soldier Schweik*, has only recently been fully translated into English. Based on Hasek's experiences in World War I, when he deserted from the Austrian army, and on his brief career as political commissar in the Red Army, *Schweik* recounts the adventures of the archetypal draft-dodging, antimilitarist "little man" as he battles in his own devious and often hilarious way the forces of stupidity, militarism, and officialdom in the crumbling Habsburg Empire. Even in inadequate translation, *Schweik* was profoundly influential on modern Western attitudes toward war, more so than its more recent American counterpart, Joseph Heller's *Catch-22*.

The trauma of World War I severely affected two other German-speaking novelists of world importance: the Swiss-German Hermann Hesse and the Austrian Robert Musil. Although he was born in Württemberg in 1877, Hesse became a Swiss citizen in 1923 following a trip to India, where both his father and grandfather had been missionaries. His experiences with the Red Cross during the war and his postwar Jungian psychoanalysis merged with his essentially religious spirit, based both on Christianity and Indian mysticism, to make him a confirmed pacifist, ascetic, and near hermit.

Like Mann, Hesse was concerned with the character and fate of the artist in the modern world, but he eventually turned to other themes in a series of lyrical, contemplative novels that won him the Nobel Prize in 1946 but that are only now attracting a vast readership, mostly among young people disillusioned with worldly stress and seeking some undefined spiritual goal. In *Steppenwolf*, Hesse pictures the artist as

Thomas Mann (above), son of a stolid Lübeck businessman and his Brazilian wife, was keenly aware of the admixture of North and South in his own blood. For him, the North represented all that was stern, industrious, and puritan; while the South embodied the sensual, the artistic, and the decadent. The apogee of Mann's anatomization of the artistic temperament is the superb novella Death in Venice, *whose artist-hero is lured south to his death by a city that is both sensuous and corrupt. Impressionist Claude Monet was equally adept at evoking Venice's fatal charms (right).*

being so alienated from society that he is, symbolically, a monstrous werewolf attempting to find reconciliation with the modern world in the "magic theatre" of his imagination. Hesse's search for spiritual order reached its fullest fruition in a mystical, Utopian novel entitled *The Glass Bead Game* that was written in 1943 but had considerable influence on American college students in the 1960's.

More seemingly conventional and less well-known, but probably a more original and powerful novelist than Hesse, was Robert Musil, who fought as an officer in World War I and then trained as an engineer, philosopher, and psychologist. After the war Musil turned his gifts exclusively to the writing of fiction, however, and in particular to *The Man Without Qualities*, which he worked on from 1930 until his death in Swiss exile in 1942. This massive work is both a *Bildungsroman* about the development of its indecisive, intellectual hero, Ulrich, and a vast *roman fleuve* on the order of *Ulysses* or *Remembrance of Things Past*. Where *Ulysses* treats life in Dublin on a single day, Musil's novel is equally exhaustive about a whole year, 1913–14, just prior to Aus-

tria's entry into the war. In exploring the shallowness, snobbery, and decadence of prewar Vienna, Musil clearly shows the roots of moral decay in the Habsburg Empire, whose inevitable death was to be hastened by the coming conflict. Since he sees Austria as locked in an inertia of sterile tradition and absurd self-aggrandizement, Musil conveys his sense of meaningless activity and cultural stagnation by means of an almost entirely plotless novel—a factor perhaps responsible for the work's failure to reach average readers. Yet *The Man Without Qualities* is a work of great philosophical introspection, technical ingenuity, and charm—one that places Musil on a level with Joyce and Proust as one of those hero-villains in the history of the novel who seem to have finished the form off by exploiting it to its ultimate limits.

After such great beginnings in the twentieth century, the German novel suffered, as was to be expected, during the Nazi years, in which only crude works of blatant propaganda could be published—unless, of course, the novelist, like Mann, Hesse, or Musil, were writing in exile and being published by neutral Swiss or Swedish German-language presses. Since art and modern dictatorships are mutually antagonistic, the German novel did not begin to function again until after World War II, but then it saw a revival at least as spectacular as postwar Germany's economic recovery, and contemporary writers are producing fiction as exciting as any in the world today.

Largely responsible for this phoenixlike recovery from the ashes are three major postwar novelists, Günter Grass, Heinrich Böll, and Uwe Johnson. Together they formed the nucleus of *Gruppe 47*, a loose association of writers who banded together in 1947 to try to rescue German literature from the havoc wrought by the Nazis. As they recognized, the German language itself had been so infiltrated and corrupted by Nazi propagandizing that it was sorely in need of purifying and revitalizing before any work of literary stature could be composed in it again, and this task they accomplished with great skill and imagination.

Grass particularly has been influential on the postwar scene, not only as a novelist and dramatist but as a graphic artist—he designs the dust jackets for his own novels—and as political propagandist. In his major work, *The Tin Drum*, first published in 1959, fantasy and realism blend to give a history of the German home front that is both harrowing and grotesquely comic. Grass's antihero, Oskar, is a childlike dwarf who has the power to drive men mad with the incessant beating on his drum, and whose picaresque adventures provide bitter satiric comment both on the Nazi mentality and bloated postwar business types seeking to forget their war guilt through the making of money.

In point of fact, this theme has been a central concern of the *Gruppe 47* novelists. Like Grass, Böll and Johnson will not permit their fellow countrymen to forget the crimes of the Nazi era, and they are equally hard on the smug material contentment they see in the postwar West German bourgeoisie. They seek a unification of Germany, but are wary of compromise with the Communist dictatorship of the East. Above all, they feel themselves, in the tradition of Goethe and Mann, committed to political action as Europeans rather than as German nationalists. In them and their followers lies the hope—already at least

Although Kafka died a decade before the Nazis came to power, his macabre fantasies were a portent of the human misery that accompanied the most devastating war in history. The Scream (above), by Edvard Munch, is equally evocative of the chaos and horror of World War II. It remained for postwar German novelists—led by Günter Grass—to pick up the pieces of a shattered literary tradition. A dramatist and graphic artist as well as a novelist (his woodcut below adorned the dust jacket of The Tin Drum), Grass blends fantasy with realism. Scandinavian novelists have never enjoyed the world prominence accorded Scandinavian playwrights; nevertheless authors such as Isak Dinesen (right) have contributed splendid fiction.

partially fulfilled—for a resurgence of the German literary spirit. The awarding of the Nobel Prize to Böll, and his giving sanctuary to his fellow Nobel laureate, Alexander Solzhenitsyn, when the latter was expelled from the Soviet Union in 1974, are acts of great symbolic promise. As soldiers on opposite sides of the Eastern Front only thirty years before, these two talented novelists might have killed each other.

In his early autobiographical novella, *Tonio Kröger*, Mann's hero, torn between his Nordic and Mediterranean heritages, reflects on "that clean, meaty, whimsical Scandinavian literature . . . there's nothing like it, I love it." Yet the Scandinavian novel has rarely achieved the world prominence that such playwrights as Ibsen and Strindberg, and such composers as Grieg and Sibelius, have enjoyed.

This is a most unfortunate situation, perhaps attesting more to the parochialism of novel-readers' tastes than to any inferiority in such writers as the Norwegians Sigrid Undset and Knut Hamsun, the Swedes Selma Lagerlöf and Pär Lagerkvist, and that Danish heiress to the magical tale-telling tradition of Hans Christian Andersen, Baroness Karen Blixen, better known as Isak Dinesen. The latter, in addition to writing such splendid stories of mystery and romance as *Seven Gothic Tales* and *Winter's Tales*, recaptured her early experiences managing a coffee plantation in Kenya in the classic *Out of Africa*, which no less an old Africa hand than Ernest Hemingway proclaimed the finest book ever written on the subject.

Sigrid Undset achieved considerable popularity and fame at one time with her trilogy about medieval Norway, *Kristin Lavransdatter*. But the vitality of both *Kristin Lavransdatter* and a later series, *The Master of Hestviken*, seems to have waned considerably since the twenties, in part because of Undset's tendency toward overdocumentation and monotony of style, in part because of the exoticism of the subject matter to non-Scandinavian readers. An Ibsen play or a Sibelius symphony give one a sense of Scandinavia more rapidly and effectively than do Undset's infinitely slow and detailed novels. A further phenomenon, which has been noticed particularly by Catholic critics, is that while the plays of Ibsen and Strindberg are antireligious, revolutionary, and distinctly modernist in tone, the great Scandinavian novelists tend to be reactionary, devout, and deeply traditional—in many cases going back to the medieval sagas in which Scandinavia was so rich for their inspiration, and that clearly this attitude ill accords with the modern, secular Western temper. Of no one was this truer than of Knut Hamsun, who was bitterly opposed to Ibsen and other liberal Norwegian writers, and whose early novel, *Hunger* (1890), and a subsequent work, *The Growth of the Soil* (1917), although deeply conservative in theme, once enjoyed wide popularity.

Sibelius once observed that while other composers were serving their audiences many-colored cocktails, he had nothing to offer but a glass of cold water. The literary equivalent of one of his austerely bracing late symphonies would be a novel by Knut Hamsun, and readers suffering from the literary hangovers induced by a *Lolita* or a *Gravity's Rainbow* might benefit from prolonged immersion in one of the great Scandinavian novelists.

9

Changing Times, Enduring Art

As HAS BEEN PREVIOUSLY INDICATED, Italy and Spain led the rest of Europe in the early production of great prose fiction. Giovanni Boccaccio practically invented the short story in his celebrated mid-fourteenth-century work, the *Decameron*; and Miguel de Cervantes Saavedra, who published *Don Quixote* at the outset of the seventeenth century, became one of the most influential, widely read, and best-loved authors of all time. Yet after this auspicious beginning, prose fiction in both countries languished until the dawn of the twentieth century, and neither country can boast the impressive catalogues of fictional masterworks produced by England, France, Russia, and the United States in the eighteenth and nineteenth centuries.

The reasons for this long novelistic drought are many and complex. Because the novel is fundamentally a social form of art, dependent on reflecting realistically the mores of its time—and because it is especially closely identified with middle-class interests—it needs a coherent, well-defined society to nurture it. Significantly, the social, political, and economic modernization that began in England and France in the early 1600's did not occur in Italy or Spain until much later, and as a result those countries failed to evolve strong novelistic traditions. The sort of middle class that emerged triumphant from England's seventeenth-century Civil War is only now emerging in Spain, for instance, and the sense of national identity that France has long enjoyed came to Italy only with the Risorgimento of the mid-nineteenth century.

Compounding this situation was the fact that aristocratic or feudal societies like those of Italy and Spain tended to prize poetry and drama above fiction. In this light it is significant that both Boccaccio and the greatest nineteenth-century Italian novelist, Alessandro Manzoni, were poets as well as novelists—and that the 1499 Spanish masterpiece, Fernando de Rojas's *La Celestina* (known in English as *The Spanish Bawd*), is a novel cast in the form of a gigantic, unperformable, twenty-one-act play. Even more inhibiting was the clerical repressiveness from which the educational systems in Spain and Italy suffered. Clergymen throughout the ages have branded fiction as sinful, but only in the Mediterranean countries were they able to impose those reactionary views on potential readers so successfully for so long a time.

Finally, because of Italy's late emergence into secular nationhood the Italian language itself had long been fragmented into countless dia-

After an auspicious beginning sparked by Giovanni Boccaccio's fourteenth-century masterpiece, the Decameron, *Italy's novelistic tradition lay dormant until the publication of Alessandro Manzoni's* The Betrothed *in 1827. Episodes from Manzoni's seminal work embellish a ceiling of the Pitti Palace in Florence.*

lects, incomprehensible from one part of the peninsula to another. Masterfully used by a Giovanni Verga in his Sicilian novels, these dialects can add spice to the language, but for a long time they prevented the writing and publication of fiction that could be understood, let alone enjoyed, nationwide. One of Manzoni's great accomplishments, therefore, lay in establishing a literary language for the writing of fiction, much as Pushkin had done in Russia.

Although Boccaccio, Verga's predecessor by almost five centuries, wrote works in Latin as well as in the vernacular, he is best remembered today for his extraordinary collection of one hundred Italian tales, the *Decameron*. In this work ten young people spend two weeks sequestered in a country villa to escape the Black Death that struck Florence in 1348. To wile away their time, each tells ten tales—tales of amorous intrigue, of pure adventure, of comedy, of tragedy. The narrators are aristocratic, but their stories cover the entire social spectrum of medieval Italian life, just as all strata of medieval English society are revealed in the tales told by Chaucer's Canterbury pilgrims. Although they are an enormously ambitious—and largely successful—undertaking, the tales in the *Decameron* suffer from a certain thinness of characterization and a repetitiousness of theme. Pure narration is Boccaccio's strongest fictional talent. Plot is all, or nearly all, yet it is doubtful that Boccaccio could have sustained interest in a long novel. As it is, he is the father of the short story—or, more properly, of what the Italians call the novella.

The real novel as we know it did not come to Italy until the early nineteenth century, ushered in by the sole fictional masterpiece of Alessandro Manzoni, *The Betrothed*. Manzoni began as a poet, his 1821 ode to Napoleon winning him a European reputation. From 1821 to 1827 he labored on *The Betrothed*, a massive historical novel influenced by Scott but more reminiscent to English readers of Charles Reade's *The Cloister and the Hearth*. Set around Milan and Lake Como in the years 1628–31, *The Betrothed* is a breathtaking account of the flight of two young peasant lovers, Renzo and Lucia, from Don Rodrigo, a locally powerful tyrant who wants Lucia for himself. After many vicissitudes Rodrigo repents, dies of the plague, and the two harassed lovers are able to marry. With quiet humor and compassion for the poor, and with penetrating historical and psychological analysis, Manzoni created a novel that won not only the hearts of Italians struggling for national unity and social justice but the admiration of such foreigners as Goethe, Poe, and Scott. Even after its initial publication, Manzoni kept working on *The Betrothed*, so that in 1840–42 a new, definitive edition brought the style into line with a truly national Italian prose understandable to all.

This was perhaps Manzoni's greatest feat. It made him a hero of the Risorgimento, and when he died in 1873, Giuseppe Verdi, long a devout admirer of the poet and novelist, composed a great requiem in his honor. Yet in its high-flown romanticism *The Betrothed* shows its age today, much as Scott's novels do, and to non-Italian readers *The Betrothed* too often reads like a glorified soap opera. This dated quality does not affect our pleasure in reading the works of Manzoni's great

As befits a Renaissance man of letters, Boccaccio is depicted at right clasping a book. His many works of prose and poetry gave Italy a literary tradition, and his Decameron *influenced all of Western literature. The one hundred tales contained in the latter range from anecdotes and fables to folk tales and fantasies, and they encompass the entire social spectrum of medieval Italy.*

DOMINVS IOHANNES BOCCACCIVS

successor, Giovanni Verga, however; indeed Verga, a Sicilian who resided for a time in Florence and in Milan, is often considered the father of modern neorealistic Italian fiction. In his short stories and such novels as *The House by the Medlar Tree* and *Mastro Don Gesualdo*, he extended the realism of Flaubert and the naturalism of Zola into the particularly Italian concept of *verismo,* or truthfulness to life, an austere, understated rendition of the brutal, minimal lives of Sicilian peasants and petty landowners.

Verga came to *verismo* in an oddly random way. He had already written several conventionally romantic popular novels when:

> I came on a ship's log, a fairly ungrammatical and unsyntactical manuscript, in which a ship's master gave succinctly an account of the various misfortunes his sailing ship had weathered. From the point of view of a mariner: without a sentence more than necessary; briefly. It struck me. I reread it: it was what I had been looking for without clearly realizing it.... It was a beam of light!

That mariner's log evidently influenced Verga the way the Code Napoléon had influenced Stendhal. At a time when such popular Italian novelists as Gabriele D'Annunzio were indulging in hyperromantic, overripe tales of perfumed passion, Verga stripped down his prose to essentials. A dramatist as well as a novelist, he employed dialogue rather than description to make his effects, which are as striking today as when they were first conceived. Like Hemingway in America and Isaac Babel in Russia, Verga demonstrated the aesthetic truth of the adage "Less is more."

Verga lived a long life, and in a way was probably fortunate to die when he did, just a few months before Mussolini's historic March on Rome on October 28, 1922, for with the advent of Fascism the kind of realism Verga practiced became politically suspect. Fascist aesthetics

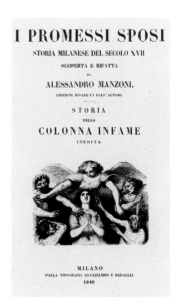

I PROMESSI SPOSI

STORIA MILANESE DEL SECOLO XVII

SCOPERTA E RIFATTA

DI

ALESSANDRO MANZONI.

EDIZIONE RIVEDUTA DALL'AUTORE

STORIA

DELLA

COLONNA INFAME

INEDITA.

MILANO

DALLA TIPOGRAFIA GUGLIELMINI E REDAELLI.

1840

Alessandro Manzoni's historical novel I Promessi Sposi, *or* The Betrothed, *enjoyed immense popularity when it was first published in 1827. But the novel did not make its real contribution to Italian literature until 1842 (title page opposite), when Manzoni further refined the Florentine dialect he had used in the earlier edition, thus giving Italy a modern literary language. Episodes from the novel, which deals with the obstacles encountered by two peasant lovers who wish to marry, are shown above.*

Overleaf: *The spare, simple room where Manzoni worked (left) contrasts sharply with the finely appointed study of his literary successor, Giovanni Verga.*

require either rosy romanticism or meretriciously heroic, larger-than-life attitudes designed to deflect the readers' attentions from the social injustices and moral squalor surrounding them. The struggle of Italian writers against this aesthetic—sometimes covert, sometimes outright—forms one of the noblest chapters in Italian literature.

One great writer who could never have survived in a Fascist state was Italo Svevo, the nom de plume—meaning "Italian Swabian"—of Ettore Schmitz. As his pen name implies, Svevo was a total cosmopolite, a writer of Italian, German, and Jewish ancestry who lived in the international city of Trieste. He was a successful, widely traveled businessman whose sensitive first novels, *A Life* and *As a Man Grows Older*, met with little recognition when they appeared in the D'Annunzio-dominated 1890's. Later, however, a most fortunate event occurred: Svevo, seeking to improve his English in order to further business relations in London, chanced to take lessons from none other than James Joyce, who was teaching English during his self-exile in Trieste. Joyce read the early novels, admired them, and befriended Svevo.

Joyce's propagandizing on Svevo's behalf, particularly for the older novelist's 1923 masterpiece, *The Confessions of Zeno*, made Svevo more famous abroad than in Italy. Not surprisingly, Svevo's businessman-hero, Zeno, resembles Joyce's own Leopold Bloom: both are lonely, deeply humane men living in a fragmented, alienated urban world; both are civilized pacifists in a world of barely concealed violence; both are too self-analytical for their own good; and both are henpecked men of more than average sensuality. Finally and most important, both are treated with immense humor and compassion.

Yet *The Confessions of Zeno* is not a pale copy of *Ulysses* but a unique and idiosyncratic masterpiece in its own right. Much of it is concerned with the hero's hilariously unavailing attempts to quit smoking, during which he keeps promising his wife and himself that each new cigarette will be his last. In 1928 the creator of this trope was

involved in a serious automobile accident and thrown from his car onto the road. As he was awaiting medical treatment, Svevo cadged a cigarette from a bystander. He lit it, exclaimed, "This really *is* my last cigarette!"—and died. The total, comic identification with his character and his art at the moment of death is pure Svevo and a symbolic triumph of committed art over mere mortality.

The civilized, humane values of Svevo somehow survived the *ventennio*, the twenty-odd-year Fascist dictatorship, thanks to the talents and courage of a number of novelists who either ignored or defied Mussolini's censors. These men—Alberto Moravia, Ignazio Silone, Elio Vittorini, Cesare Pavese, and many more—represent an explosion of fictional talent during and immediately after the war years, one which showed that Italy, in her political agony, had at least attained her place in the novelistic sun. In many cases these novelists first came to the attention of foreigners because of the contemporaneous—and related—explosion of neorealistic films in the years just after World War II, years when a devastated Italy nevertheless managed to produce such works of haunting power and deep-grained humanity as *Open City*, *Shoeshine*, *Paisan*, and *The Bicycle Thief*. In some cases the writers actually participated in making the films; in others, novelist and filmmaker simply shared a common vision of life.

This modern point of view was first enunciated as far back as 1929 by Alberto Moravia in his novel *The Time of Indifference*, which aroused Fascist enmity by its bleak, unsparing portrait of the moral corruption and spiritual aridity of Italian bourgeois life. Mussolini himself was purportedly enraged by the scathing portrait of a dictator contained in Moravia's *Fancy Dress Ball*—but Italy was not Germany, and the author Moravia managed to survive. His books were censored or went unpublished and unreviewed, and as late as 1952 his entire works were placed on the Catholic Index of Forbidden Books, but nonetheless he survived.

Moravia's somewhat inflated international fame came after the war. It was based upon his grimly realistic account of a prostitute's life, *Woman of Rome*, and was furthered by distinguished and popular motion pictures based on a brace of his better novels, *Two Women* and *The Conformist*. If more recent Italian writers like Italo Calvino and Tommaso Landolfi have turned away from Moravia it is because there is a certain monotonous repetitiveness to his work; he seems to have run the realist well dry. In much the same way, later Italian film directors such as Michelangelo Antonioni and Federico Fellini have turned their backs on the earlier neorealism of Roberto Rosselini and Vittorio de Sica for a more stylized, phantasmagoric rendition of experience.

Perhaps the most potent anti-Fascist novelist was Ignazio Silone, the pen name of Secondo Tranquilli. Certainly there is nothing either secondary or tranquil about Silone's finest novels, written in Swiss exile: *Fontamara* (1933) and *Bread and Wine* (1937). Both extol the enduring virtues of stoicism and independence displayed by the Italian peasantry under Fascist rule. At first glance these novels of rural deprivation seem typical of the Marxist social realism of the 1930's, and in fact Silone was a Communist for a time. But neither *Fontamara* nor *Bread and Wine* ever falls into stale propagandizing through stereotypical characters, and their humor and lyricism have endured well past the "Red decade," justifying Albert Camus's accolade: "Silone speaks to the whole of Europe."

Another heterodox Communist whose reputation has grown with every year since his suicide in 1950 is Cesare Pavese, perhaps the finest artist in fiction produced by modern Italy. Pavese and his friend, the similarly gifted Elio Vittorini, began their careers as translators of British and American fiction for the Turin publishing house of Einaudi. Vittorini learned English by painstakingly translating *Robinson Crusoe*, word by word, from a dictionary; the better-educated Pavese had written a doctoral dissertation on Walt Whitman. By and large, Fascist authorities encouraged such translations, hoping that the starkly realistic picture of the underside of American life presented by the novels of Dos Passos and Steinbeck would make Italians better appreciate their own society. The scheme backfired, however, for readers hailed the honesty permitted fiction in a free society.

The experience of translating Defoe, Dickens, Melville, Joyce, and Faulkner gave Pavese a sophistication in the handling of fiction almost unique in his generation. His nine novels are brief but pungent expressions of the anomie of modern life, usually among the upper-middle-class and aristocratic denizens of the great manufacturing city of Turin. *Among Women Only* stands out as perhaps his masterpiece, and it provided the script for Antonioni's first mature film, *Le Amiche*. Pavese's suicide—allegedly the result of an unhappy love affair with an American actress—was to rob Italy of one of its subtlest modern novelists.

We began this journey through the world of fiction with Samuel Richardson seated in a pleasant suburban garden, giving advice to a bevy of lovelorn girls and conceiving the idea for *Pamela*, the first English novel. We must end with a very different scene: a filthy Spanish prison where Miguel de Cervantes Saavedra is immured for alleged frauds committed while collecting money to supply the ill-fated Armada of 1588. Cervantes is surrounded by rats, not admirers, but he is writing perhaps the greatest and certainly the most influential novel of all time, *The Ingenious Gentleman Don Quixote de la Mancha*.

The differing circumstances underlying the creation of the English and the Spanish novel are both literarily and symbolically significant. Where England has always provided fertile soil—to say nothing of freedom—for her novelists, the Spanish earth, as Ernest Hemingway once said in a different context, is dry and hard. Where Richardson's beginnings, brilliant as they are, were only tentative explorations of some of the possibilities of fiction, possibilities that would be more fully developed in two hundred years of ceaseless creativity, Cervantes' novel seems to have been not merely a beginning but an ending as well. No Spanish novelist has written anything remotely as fine since *Don Quixote*. It contains, often in full fruition, the seeds of all future fiction —from Henry Fielding, who pounced on it eagerly as the model of picaresque fiction, to Saul Bellow, whose greatest novel could as easily have been given the title *The Ingenious Would-Be Gentleman Augie March of Chicago*.

The novels of Gabriele D'Annunzio (above, left) are characterized by lushness of language and intensity of emotion but marred by melodrama. His The Flame of Life, *inspired by the author's love affair with actress Eleonora Duse (left, below), caused an international scandal when it was published in 1900. The undisputed leader of the neorealist school of writing that emerged in Italy after World War II is Alberto Moravia (below). For Moravia, worldwide recognition came with publication of* Woman of Rome, *his brutal account of a prostitute's life, and the release of two highly acclaimed motion pictures based upon a pair of his better novels,* Two Women *and* The Conformist.

These differences were not merely stylistic, of course. Richardson led the placid life of one of eighteenth-century England's new-rich bourgeoisie, whereas Cervantes' life was packed with swashbuckling, often disastrous, adventure. He lost the use of his left hand fighting in the Battle of Lepanto. There he was captured by the Turks and sent in slavery to Algiers. He attempted to escape four times, was finally ransomed, wrote some plays and short novels, became a tax collector, and consequently landed—several times—in jail. When the first part of *Don Quixote* was published in 1605 his name became a byword throughout Spain, but Cervantes never made much money and he managed to complete the second part of his masterpiece only a short time before his death on April 23, 1616—the very day of Shakespeare's death.

Where Richardson's genius was confined to the mores of domestic life, Cervantes' incorporated all of Spain, socially as well as geographically, from the meanest swineherd to the most mincing aristocrat. Richardson's surface realism is a minor triumph when compared to the profound realism of Cervantes, whose novel, so realistic that you can practically smell Spain on every page, nevertheless deals with such abstract, metaphysical concepts as the difference between appearance and reality, between sanity and madness, between the flesh and the spirit, between art and life. In the complementary figures of Don Quixote and Sancho Panza, Cervantes captured all of humanity for all time. Without them, would we have Pickwick and Sam Weller, Tom Sawyer and Huck Finn, or even Sherlock Holmes and Dr. Watson?

The problem for the Spanish novel, then, was what it could do for an encore. The answer, sadly, was not much, and indeed the Spanish literary genius has been devoted almost exclusively to poetry and drama. As one critic, Harriet de Onís, has pointed out, the naturalism so important to the growth of the novel in nineteenth-century Europe is inimical to the Spanish temperament, which abhors the "cold, detached scientific observation" such writing requires. Thus, in the nineteenth century, when the European novel was enjoying its golden age, Spanish writers were concentrating on *costumbrismo*, novels of local color celebrating the way of life in one region of Spain or another with dismaying emphasis on picturesque externals—castanets, mantillas, bullfights—rather than the inner lives of richly conceived characters.

One Spanish novelist of the nineteenth century does stand out, however. He is Benito Pérez Galdós, whom most Spaniards regard as Dickens, Balzac, and Tolstoy all rolled into one. Certainly his immense productivity was Balzacian: one cycle of novels alone comes to forty-six volumes, and his masterpiece, *Fortunata and Jacinta* (1886–87), is an epic treatment of life in Madrid that is only slightly shorter than *War and Peace*. Yet Pérez Galdós has never made the impact on the non-Hispanic world that he clearly deserves, with the effect that those who do not read Spanish can never hope fully to make his acquaintance.

The same might be said of other locally famous Spanish novelists who do not seem to travel very well and who, if they have become celebrated outside Spain, are usually valued for extrinsic reasons. For example, Pedro Antonio de Alarcón, a contemporary of Pérez Galdós, is known to music lovers for his novella *The Three-Cornered Hat*

Miguel de Cervantes Saavedra (above) began writing his masterpiece, Don Quixote, *while in prison for fraud. Some 350 years later, his picaresque tale of the Knight of the Sad Countenance (right, as imagined by Daumier) and his squire Sancho Panza remains the most profound study ever made of the Spanish character.*

because Manuel de Falla composed a ballet and Hugo Wolf an opera based on it. And Vicente Blasco Ibáñez, the closest equivalent Spain has to the French realists of the late nineteenth century, was once popular for his *Four Horsemen of the Apocalypse*, adapted into a famous silent motion picture to suit the steamy talents of Rudolph Valentino.

Pío Baroja, the finest Spanish novelist of the twentieth century, wrote several novels of direct, almost fiercely apprehended action somewhat analagous to Hemingway's. But more than three decades of the Franco dictatorship in Spain effectively stifled a tradition of fictional creativity that was never too healthy in the best of times. Much happier is the extraordinary outgrowth of novels produced in Latin American countries since World War II. After long years of struggling for cultural as well as economic independence from Europe, of battling almost universal illiteracy, lack of native publishing houses, and censorship—years during which native writers produced essentially derivative copies of European fictional realism—the Spanish American novelists has, in recent times, come splendidly into his own. Such older writers as the Argentinian Jorge Luis Borges, the Nobel Prize-winning Guatamalan Miguel Angel Asturias, the Cuban Alejo Carpentier, and the Argentinian Julio Cortázar—joined by such younger talents as the Peruvian Mario Vargas Llosa and the Colombian Gabriel García Márquez—have made vital contributions to world fiction and are among the most exciting novelists writing today.

How have they accomplished this feat in defiance of the repressive regimes most of them, at one time or another, have lived under? Some, like Borges and Cortázar, have of course done much of their writing in exile. But almost all of them have also adopted a style of writing known as *realismo mágico*, or "magic realism," that enables them both to avoid censorship and to explore new avenues in fiction that are of vast significance even to novelists living in more open societies. Developed in the 1920's out of such European modernist phenomena as Dadaism and Surrealism, magic realism took on a peculiarly South American local coloration by the 1940's. If life in South America was too bizarre to be treated with conventional realism, these writers felt, why not give it its head and treat it with appropriately mythic, magical, and dreamlike techniques? However well the drabness of life in Flaubert's Rouen or Bennett's Five Towns suited their techniques of documentary realism, such an approach ill-accorded with a world of lush rain forests teeming with weird flora and fauna, of conflicting Indian and Spanish cultures, of savagely unstable politics, of ominous gulfs between the very rich and the very poor.

By jettisoning an already outworn realism, twentieth-century Latin American novelists placed a new reliance on such ingredients as Indian legends, complex metaphysical allegories, and cinematic techniques of narration. By no means a minor benefit of this new style of writing was that in its subtle allusiveness and imaginative complexity it completely dumbfounded censors, never the most sophisticated of readers. Thus, for example, in the fables of Borges and Cortázar statements could be made about the evils of the Perón regime in Argentina that would never pass censors if presented in terms of the surface realism of the past.

The Spanish novelistic tradition begun by Cervantes has withered under the repressive Franco dictatorship in Spain but flowered in the Spanish-speaking countries of Latin America. Argentinians Jorge Luis Borges (above) and Julio Cortázar (right, above), Nobel Prize-winning Guatamalan Miguel Angel Asturias (right, below), and Colombian Gabriel García Márquez (below) are among the most exciting novelists writing today.

146

This is not to say that politics is the only major concern of South American novelists. Many of them are fascinated by the contrast in their lands between primeval jungle and supermodern city life. In *The Lost Steps*, by the Cuban musicologist Alejo Carpentier, a sophisticated, Europeanized musician searching for primitive instruments in the Orinoco region finds instead his own roots in the jungle; like Carpentier himself, he is in search of the *real maravilloso*, or "marvelous reality," that still exists in vast areas of South America in defiance of the encroaching drabness of urban civilization.

Similarly, in perhaps the most brilliant of recent South American novels, *A Hundred Years of Solitude* by Gabriel García Márquez, an entire fictional world is established in the depths of the jungle by the highly eccentric Buendía family. In its total, Edenesque isolation, the history of Macondo reproduces, in allegorical microcosm, the course of all civilizations from innocence through experience to decadence and dissolution. A highly ambitious program for a novel, but Márquez carries it off brilliantly, thanks largely to a style as dense in its poetic suggestiveness as the tropical jungle he writes about.

Not all Latin American novelists choose to write on the epic scale of a Márquez or a Llosa, whose *The Green House* is another elaborate parable of primitivism versus civilization. Perhaps the writer who has had the greatest impact on fiction outside his native Argentina is the scholarly poet, critic, and translator Jorge Luis Borges, whose finest works are the very short stories contained in his *Fictions* and *The Aleph*. By translating sections of *Ulysses* as early as 1925, Borges brought a realization of the potentialities of modern fictional prose to his fellow South Americans. He also lectured on Anglo-Saxon literature at Buenos Aires University and, in spite of ever-encroaching blindness, read and mastered most of the world's literatures. Like Joyce, he may literally have read himself blind in his passion for the written word.

Borges was a respected librarian in Buenos Aires when, in 1946, the Perón regime reduced him to the civil service rank of chicken inspector. Apart from the outrageous insult, there is something to that symbolic act that might have appealed to the highly original sense of humor of a man capable of writing a brief but moving prose poem about his toenails. For Borges's originality consists of his seeing unique facets of experience denied to other authors equipped with better physical eyesight. In his blindness, Borges turns his vision inward and produces small-scale masterpieces of metaphysical wit and terror comparable only to the cryptic apothegms of Kafka or the eerily intricate paintings of Paul Klee. In other ways, his mythic imagination goes right back to *Don Quixote*.

From the imprisonment of Cervantes to the chicken inspectorship of Borges, the novelist writing in Spanish has never had an easy time of it. Too often he has had to perfect his art in spiritual isolation from the rest of the world, under a regime profoundly hostile to any productions of the free imagination, for a limited and harassed readership. It is a tribute to the enduring human spirit that these novelists have been able to write at all, let alone produce a *Don Quixote* or a *Hundred Years of Solitude*.

10

After Cervantes

In the summer of 1889, while he was engaged in his literary conquest of London, Henry James received a request from the Deerfield, Massachusetts summer school, inviting the author to attend a symposium on the future of the novel. James sent his regrets, but in the same letter he addressed a few words on the subject to the "nymphs and swains" he envisioned seated "under the great trees at Deerfield." This is part of what he had to say:

> To tell the truth, I can't help thinking that we already talk too much about the novel, about and around it, in proportion to the quantity of it having any importance that we produce. . . . Oh, do something from your point of view . . . do something with life. . . . The field is vast for freedom, for study, for observation, for satire, for truth. . . . Every sort of mind will find what it looks for in it, whereby the novel becomes truly multifarious and illustrative. That is what I mean by liberty; give it its head and let it range. If it is in a bad way . . . nothing but absolute freedom can refresh it and restore its self-respect.

So, nearly a century ago, the great idealist, theorist, and practitioner of the novel, granting that the form was "in a bad way" yet rather fed up with premature elegies for it, expressed his faith that "the great form" was still sufficiently capacious to be filled by any number of fresh new talents, each seeing life from his own peculiar angle of vision, his unique point of view. James knew there are as many potential novels as there are individual human beings.

How relevant does James's faith in the future of the novel appear today, long after seemingly conclusive experiments in the form have been made by such novelists as James Joyce and Virginia Woolf—and by James himself; when magazines publishing fiction have nearly all gone out of business; when book publishers regard novels with the same anxiety or contempt formerly reserved for slim volumes of esoteric poetry; when most readers proudly say they "have no time" for reading fiction? In the first half of the twentieth century the theater came to be regarded as "the fabulous invalid." Is the novel, as critics are daily telling us, the illustrious deceased?

Certainly James's "great form" has been fecund and multifarious in the past. Infinitely plastic, protean, expandable, and contractable, it has

The well-stocked shelves of the Scribner Book Store in New York are but one indication that the novel is alive and well in the twentieth century.

equally suited a Dostoevsky and a P. G. Wodehouse, produced an *Emma* and a *Huckleberry Finn*, inspired a Flaubert, a Goethe, a Melville. But forms, too, can flourish and die; few today would undertake to write a Japanese Noh play or a Monteverdian madrigal. Have novelists, then, echoed Thackeray's lament at the end of *Vanity Fair* and "shut up the box and the puppets" because their "play is played out"?

Certainly novels continue to be produced in vast quantities. But when the need for a form, its *raison d'être*, has disappeared, the works being written in it come to us like the cold light from a long-dead star, a star so remote that the news of its death has not yet filtered through the universe. Presumably one could write a classical sonata today, or build a baroque church, but it would lack the spirit of the age to give it genuine aesthetic life. Similarly, why write an epistolary novel when we already have *Clarissa*—and no one writes letters anymore, anyway? Or a *Bildungsroman* when we already have *Portrait of the Artist* and *The Magic Mountain?* Or a novel of scrupulous social observation when the very forms and conventions of society that gave meaning to every gesture in *Middlemarch* and *Anna Karenina* have long vanished from the scene? It could be done, but no novelist worthy of the name ever deliberately set out to write a museum piece.

The very word "novel" means "news," and each generation gets its news in different ways. Philip Roth has complained that the nature of real news in our day is so staggeringly grotesque that it has exceeded the wildest fantasy and invaded what used to be the novelist's exclusive territory. (A case in point: A special "Watergate Edition" of Roth's *Our Gang* had to be prepared when his satiric fantasy about the Nixon administration was overtaken by actual events more bizarre than those the author had imagined.) The grimmest paranoid nightmares of a Kafka became daily occurrences, less than twenty years after his death, in the concentration camps of Nazi Germany; and we daily see Orwell's *1984* drawing closer with the speed of light and the inexorability of a steamroller. If one picture is worth a thousand words, perhaps one newspaper today is worth a thousand novels.

Novelists have responded to this situation in a variety of ways. One has been to write what Truman Capote calls the nonfiction novel and what others have called pop journalism or parajournalism. The application of fictional techniques to actual events has also occupied the time and talents of Norman Mailer, who in earlier times probably would have been exclusively concerned with writing novels. In the hands of a Mailer or a Capote such books make exciting reading, but they are ultimately a confession of the bankruptcy not only of the novel but of journalism as well.

The current preference of most readers for nonfiction has produced yet another literary aberration: the novel so concentrated on informing the reader about a particular industry or country that its purely fictional content amounts to only the thinnest sugarcoating on the factual pill the novelist is serving up. Such popular successes as James Michener's *Hawaii* and Arthur Hailey's *Hotel* give the reader the illusion that he is learning something about a country's history or the inner workings of a complex industry, rather than wasting his time with mere pure fiction. They are usually extensively researched and indeed informative, but not necessarily about the human condition.

Such works are essentially for readers too lazy to study history for themselves, readers who need some sort of narrative line, no matter how anemic or implausible, to keep them going. They are a boon to novelists who need the props of research to project their art into the real world because they cannot present a richly imagined world of their own. No one would read *Moby Dick* primarily to learn about the whaling industry—it has more important things to tell us about ourselves. Conversely no one would read *Wheels* for a unique vision of man's place in the cosmos—if we don't learn about the automobile industry from it, we have learned nothing. In the orginal sense of the word "novel," such novels have no import.

The Einsteinian experiments in narrative technique carried out so brilliantly by Joyce and Proust in the first half of the twentieth century have led to another ominous development in the novel's modern history. Bored by conventional means of storytelling, these and other innovators brought such complexity to the narrative art that, while they have excited other novelists and connoisseurs of the novel, they have at the same time alienated the mass audience of readers who once so eagerly awaited the latest production of a Dickens or an Arnold Bennett. The estrangement between the serious artist and his public that has marked all the arts in the twentieth century has been almost as destructive for the novel as for painting and music. Baffled by the sophisticated techniques of the modern masters of fiction, many readers have turned to such subgenres of the novel as the detective story or science fiction, where conventional methods of plotting, characterization, and handling of chronology still prevail.

But the greatest challenge to the novel in our time has been the movies and television. They have sapped the novel of its unique strength and stolen its producers and readers as devastatingly as they have stolen playwrights and the audience for plays. Many writers who in earlier times would have been novelists or dramatists have instead given their talents to the cinema, which is clearly the most vital—and lucrative—indigenous art form of the twentieth century. A movie like *Citizen Kane*, or a television series like *The Mary Tyler Moore Show*, is doing, with immense skill in a fresh medium, what the novel was doing as recently as fifty years ago.

Yet movies are very different from novels—a truth underscored by the fact that the better the novel a movie is based on, the poorer the movie—with the best movies stemming from ideas originally conceived for the medium. Fictional masterpieces like *The Great Gatsby*, handled with the greatest possible tact, care, and affection, become cinematic disasters, while as tawdry a concept as the one underlying *Casablanca*, which would at best result in the sort of novel meant to be read under a hairdryer, yields cinematic gold.

So the similarities between the novel and the movie can be deceptive. Movies move rapidly; the longest of them go by in a flash compared to the length of time it takes to read even the shortest novel. The sheer length permissable in a novel allows for such extra benefits as the comic digressions of a Sterne, the historical ruminations of a Tolstoy, and above all for the long-term immersion of the reader in the novelist's peculiar world that permit us to know the people in a long book far better than we can know the people in any movie, and even better than we may know many of our lifelong friends.

The novel has the further advantage that the reader can go back at will to any page he wishes to reread for fuller comprehension or enjoyment; the filmgoer has to see the entire movie over again to get the same effect. Novels are also wonderfully portable, and they are wonderfully private as well; you can read a novel in solitary splendor, undisturbed by the gabbers, neckers, and popcorn munchers who constitute the bulk of any given movie audience.

Most important, the movie and television experience is basically a passive one; the reading experience an active one calling for a greater alertness and imaginative empathy on the part of the reader than a movie requires from the viewer, with rewards commensurate with the investment of effort. If only a couple of generations of moviegoing has so atrophied our imaginative attention spans that we find even the worst movies more rewarding than the best novels, then the novel will truly and finally become extinct.

Until films came along, the novel, with its origins in the eighteenth century, was the newest major art form. Its rise paralleled the rise of a new, literate middle class, and spelled the doom of such literary genres as the epic, the masque, the romance, and the sermon. It is entirely possible that the novel will die with the death of the very concepts of middle-classness and of literacy and that future generations will find instruction and delight not only in talkies, but also in the "feelies" Aldous Huxley predicted in *Brave New World*, to say nothing of whatever future art forms technology may have up its sleeve for us.

Yet ultimately there is nothing new under the sun, nor has there ever been. The basic human condition remains the same, except that each artist sees it differently, and the novel has shown, in its brief life span, extraordinary flexibility in presenting that condition to us. The esotericism of Proust in the twentieth century is no more inordinately sensitive, mandarin, and complex than the sensibility of Lady Murasaki, writing her massive *Tale of Genji* in eleventh-century Japan. That early, exhaustive exploration of the nuances of social behavior and the secrets of the heart did not prevent Proust, however, from writing *Remembrance of Things Past*. The experiments of Joyce in the twentieth century were similarly anticipated by Sterne in the eighteenth. The picaresque triumph of *Don Quixote* did not prevent Fielding from writing *Tom Jones*. And even the epistolary novel, seemingly the deadest of subgenres since the eighteenth century, showed new life in Ring Lardner's *You Know Me, Al* and John O'Hara's *Pal Joey*. If we have learned one thing from the history of the novel it is that as long as the human imagination functions, and as long as we show the slightest interest in the behavior and destinies of ourselves and our fellow creatures, the novel will find ways to express this imagination and to feed this interest. It would be a mistake to toll the knell for an art form so persistently alive.

GREAT BEGINNINGS

How to begin? That vexing question, confronted by every novelist many times in his career, has been answered in every imaginable manner in the more than two hundred years since Samuel Richardson penned the opening lines of Pamela. *Only a relatively small number of authors have hit upon satisfactory solutions to the common dilemma of how to best capture the reader's imagination, fix the scene, and introduce the novel's central themes—and only a handful of these have done so with any consistency. Great novelists have frequently failed in this regard despite their formidable talents, while minor novelists have, from time to time, succeeded despite their obvious limitations. Great novels—Leo Tolstoy's* War and Peace, *for example—have often begun on a muted note, whereas lesser works—Lawrence Durrell's* Justine, *for instance—have sometimes struck a resounding opening chord. On rare occasions a writer has answered the question of how to begin with such power, felicity, and distinction that the resulting novel's opening lines have achieved a fame independent of the work itself. What follows is a representative selection of noteworthy solutions. Each is identified, but none really needs to be.*

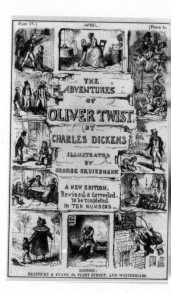

The title page above, and those on the following pages, is from a work by England's greatest novelist, Charles Dickens.

It is a truth universally acknowledged, that a single man in possession of a good fortune must be in want of a wife. However little known the feelings or views of such a man may be on his first entering a neighborhood, this truth is so well fixed in the minds of the surrounding families, that he is considered as the rightful property of some one or other of their daughters.

"My dear Mr. Bennet," said his lady to him one day, "have you heard that Netherfield Park is let at last?"

Mr. Bennet replied that he had not.

"But it is," returned she; "for Mrs. Long has just been here, and she told me all about it."

Mr. Bennet made no answer.

"Do not you want to know who has taken it?" cried his wife impatiently.

"*You* want to tell me, and I have no objection to hearing it."

This was invitation enough.

"Why, my dear, you must know, Mrs. Long says that Netherfield is taken by a young man of large fortune from the north of England; that he came down on Monday in a chaise and four to see the place, and was so much delighted with it, that he agreed with Mr. Morris immediately; that he is to take possession before Michaelmas, and some of his servants are to be in the house by the end of next week."

"What is his name?"

"Bingley."

"Is he married or single?"

"Oh! single, my dear, to be sure! A single man of large fortune; four of five thousand a-year. What a fine thing for our girls!"

"How so? how can it affect them?"

"My dear Mr. Bennet," replied his wife, "how can you be so tiresome! you must know that I am thinking of his marrying one of them."

"Is that his design in settling here?"

"Design! nonsense, how can you talk so! But it is very likely that he *may* fall in love with one of them, and therefore you must visit him as soon as he comes."

"I see no occasion for that. You and the girls may go, or you may send them by themselves, which perhaps will be still better, for as you are as handsome as any of them, Mr. Bingley might like you the best of the party."

"My dear, you flatter me. I certainly *have* had my share of beauty, but I do not pretend to be anything extraordinary now. When a woman has five grown-up daughters, she ought to give over thinking of her own beauty."

"In such cases, a woman has not often much beauty to think of."

"But, my dear, you must indeed go and see Mr. Bingley when he comes into the neighborhood."

"It is more than I engage for, I assure you."

"But consider your daughters. Only think what an establishment it would be for one of them. Sir William and Lady Lucas are determined to go, merely on that account, for in general, you know, they visit no newcomers. Indeed you must go, for it will be impossible for *us* to visit him if you do not."

"You are over-scrupulous, surely. I dare say Mr. Bingley will be very glad to see you; and I will send a few lines by you to assure him of my hearty consent to his marrying whichever he chooses of the girls: though I must throw in a good word for my little Lizzy."

"I desire you will do no such thing. Lizzy is not a bit better than the others; and I am sure she is not half so handsome as Jane, nor half so good-humored as Lydia. But you are always giving *her* the preference."

"They have none of them much to recommend them," replied he; "they are all silly and ignorant, like other girls: but Lizzy has something more of quickness than her sisters."

"Mr. Bennet, how can you abuse your own children in such a way! You take delight in vexing me. You have no compassion on my poor nerves."...

Mr. Bennet was so odd a mixture of quick parts, sarcastic humor, reserve, and caprice, that the experience of three-and-twenty years had been insufficient to make his wife understand his character. *Her* mind was less difficult to develop. She was a woman of mean understanding, little information, and uncertain temper. When she was discontented, she fancied herself nervous. The business of her life was to get her daughters married; its solace was visiting and news.

JANE AUSTEN
Pride and Prejudice, 1813

Call me Ishmael. Some years ago—never mind how long precisely—having little or no money in my purse, and nothing particular to interest me on shore, I thought I would sail about a little and see the watery part of the world. It is a way I have of driving off the spleen and regulating the circulation. Whenever I find myself growing grim about the mouth; whenever it is damp, drizzly November in my soul; whenever I find myself involuntarily pausing before coffin warehouses, and bringing up the rear of every funeral I meet; and especially whenever my hypos get such an upper hand of me, that it requires a strong moral principle to prevent me from deliberately stepping into the street, and methodically knocking people's hats off—then, I account it high time to go to sea as soon as I can. This is my substitute for pistol and ball. With a philosophical flourish Cato throws himself upon his sword; I quietly take to the ship. There is nothing surprising in this. If they but knew it, almost all men in their degree, some time or other, cherish very nearly the same feelings towards the ocean with me.

There now is your insular city of the Manhattoes, belted round by wharves as Indian isles by coral reefs—commerce surrounds it with her surf. Right and left, the streets take you waterward. Its extreme downtown is the battery, where that noble mole is washed by waves, and cooled by breezes, which a few hours previous were out of sight of land. Look at the crowds of water-gazers there.

Circumambulate the city of a dreamy Sabbath afternoon. Go from Corlears Hook to Coenties Slip, and from thence, by Whitehall, northward. What do you see?—Posted like silent sentinels all around the town, stand thousands upon thousands of mortal men fixed in ocean reveries. Some leaning against the spiles; some seated upon the pier-heads; some looking over the bulwarks of ships from China; some high aloft in the rigging, as if striving to get a still better seaward peep. But these are all landsmen; of week days pent up in lath and plaster—tied to counters, nailed to benches, clinched to desks. How then is this? Are the green fields gone? What do they here?

But look! here come more crowds, pacing straight for the water, and seemingly bound for a dive. Strange! Nothing will content them but the extremest limit of the land; loitering under the shady lee of yonder warehouses will not suffice. No. They must get as nigh the water as they possibly can without falling in. And there they stand—miles of them—leagues. Inlanders all, they come from lanes and alleys, streets and avenues—north, east, south, and west. Yet here they all unite. Tell me, does the magnetic virtue of the needles of the compasses of all those ships attract them thither?

Once more. Say you are in the country; in some high land of lakes. Take almost any path you please, and ten to one it carries you down in a dale, and leaves you there by a pool in the stream. There is magic in it. Let the most absent-minded of men be plunged in his deepest reveries—stand that man on his legs, set his feet a-going, and he will infallibly lead you to water, if water there be in all that region. Should you ever be athirst in the great American desert, try this experiment, if your caravan happen to be supplied with a metaphysical professor. Yes, as every one knows, meditation and water are wedded for ever. . . .

Now, when I say that I am in the habit of going to sea whenever I begin to grow hazy about the eyes, and begin to be over conscious of my lungs, I do not mean to have it inferred that I ever go to sea as a passenger. For to go as a passenger you must needs have a purse, and a purse is but a rag unless you have something in it. Besides, passengers get sea-sick—grow quarrelsome—don't sleep of nights—do not enjoy themselves much, as a general thing;—no, I never go as a passenger; nor, though I am something of a salt, do I ever go to sea as a Commodore, or a Captain, or a Cook. I abandon the glory and distinction of such offices to those who like them. For my part, I abominate all honorable respectable toils, trials, and tribulations of every kind whatsoever. It is quite as much as I can do to take care of myself, without taking care of ships, barques, brigs, schooners, and what not. And as for going as cook,—though I confess there is considerable glory in that, a cook being a sort of officer on ship-board—yet, somehow, I never fancied broiling fowls. . . .

No, when I go to sea, I go as a simple sailor, right before the mast, plumb down into the fore-castle, aloft there to the royal mast-head. True, they rather order me about some, and make me jump from spar to spar, like a grasshopper in a May meadow. And at first, this sort of thing is unpleasant enough. It touches one's sense of honor, particularly if you come of an old established family in the land, the Van Rensselaers, or Randolphs, or Hardicanutes. And more than all, if just previous to putting your hand into the tarpot, you have been lording it as a country schoolmaster, making the tallest boys stand in awe of you. The transition is a keen one, I assure you, from a schoolmaster to a sailor, and requires a strong decoction of Seneca and the Stoics to enable you to grin and bear it. But even this wears off in time. . . .

Again, I always go to sea as a sailor, because they make a point of paying me for my trouble, whereas they never pay passengers a single penny that I ever heard of. On the contrary, passengers themselves must pay. And there is all the difference in the world between paying and being paid. The act of paying is perhaps the most uncomfortable infliction that the two orchard thieves entailed upon us. But *being paid*, —what will compare with it? The urbane activity with which a man receives money is really marvellous, considering that we so earnestly believe money to be the root of all earthly ills, and that on no account can a monied man enter heaven. Ah! how cheerfully we consign ourselves to perdition!

Finally, I always go to sea as a sailor, because of the wholesome exercise and pure air of the fore-castle deck. For as in this world, head winds are far more prevalent than winds from astern (that is, if you never violate the Pythagorean maxim), so for the most part the Commodore on the quarter-deck gets his atmosphere at second hand from the sailors on the forecastle. He thinks he breathes it first; but not so. In much the same way do the commonalty lead their leaders in many other things, at the same time that the leaders little suspect it. But wherefore it was that after having repeatedly smelt the sea as a merchant sailor, I should now take it into my head to go on a whaling voyage; this the invisible police officer of the Fates, who has the constant surveillance of me, and secretly dogs me, and influences me in some unaccountable way—he can better answer than any one else. And, doubtless, my going on this whaling voyage, formed part of the grand programme of Providence that was drawn up a long time ago. It came in as a sort of brief interlude and solo between more extensive performances. I take it that this part of the bill must have run something like this:

"*Grand Contested Election for the Presidency of the United States.*
"WHALING VOYAGE BY ONE ISHMAEL.
"BLOODY BATTLE IN AFFGHANISTAN."

Though I cannot tell why it was exactly that those stage managers, the Fates, put me down for this shabby part of a whaling voyage, when others were set down for magnificent parts in high tragedies, and short and easy parts in genteel comedies, and jolly parts in farces—though I cannot tell why this was exactly; yet, now that I recall all the circumstances, I think I can see a little into the springs and motives which being cunningly presented to me under various disguises, induced me to set about performing the part I did, besides cajoling me into the delusion that it was a choice resulting from my own unbiased freewill and discriminating judgment.

Chief among these motives was the overwhelming idea of the great whale himself. Such a portentous and mysterious monster roused all my curiosity. Then the wild and distant seas where he rolled his island bulk; the undeliverable, nameless perils of the whale; these, with all the attending marvels of a thousand Patagonian sights and sounds, helped to sway me to my wish. With other men, perhaps, such things would not have been inducements; but as for me, I am tormented with an everlasting itch for things remote. I love to sail forbidden seas, and land on barbarous coasts. Not ignoring what is good, I am quick to perceive a horror, and could still be social with it—would they let me—since it is but well to be on friendly terms with all the inmates of the place one lodges in.

By reason of these things, then, the whaling voyage was welcome; the great flood-gates of the wonder-world swung open, and in the wild conceits that swayed me to my purpose, two and two there floated into my inmost soul, endless processions of the whale, and, mid most of them all, one grand hooded phantom, like a snow hill in the air.

HERMAN MELVILLE
Moby Dick, 1851

It was the best of times, it was the worst of times, it was the age of wisdom, it was the age of foolishness, it was the epoch of belief, it was the epoch of incredulity, it was the season of Light, it was the season of Darkness, it was the spring of hope, it was the winter of despair, we had everything before us, we had nothing before us, we were all going direct to Heaven, we were all going direct the other way—in short, the period was so far like the present period, that some of its noisiest authorities insisted on its being received, for good or for evil, in the superlative degree of comparison only.

There were a king with a large jaw and a queen with a plain face, on the throne of England; there were a king with a large jaw and a queen with a fair face, on the throne of France. In both countries it was clearer than crystal to the Lords of the State preserves of loaves and fishes, that things in general were settled forever.

It was the year of Our Lord one thousand seven hundred and seventy-five. Spiritual revelations were conceded to England at that favored period, as at this. Mrs. Southcott had recently attained her five-and-twentieth blessed birth-day, of whom a prophetic private in the Life Guards had heralded the sublime appearance by announcing that arrangements were made for the swallowing up of London and Westminister. Even the Cock-lane ghost had been laid only a round dozen of years, after rapping out its messages, as the spirits of this very year last past (supernaturally deficient in originality) rapped out theirs. Mere messages in the earthly order of events had lately come to the English Crown and People, from a Congress of British subjects in America; which, strange to relate, have proved more important to the human race than any communications yet received through any of the chickens of the Cock-lane brood.

France, less favored on the whole as to matters spiritual than her sister of the shield and trident, rolled with exceeding smoothness down hill, making paper-money and spending it. Under the guidance of her Christian pastors, she entertained herself, besides, with such humane achievements as sentencing a youth to have his hands cut off, his tongue torn out with pincers, and his body burned alive, because he had not kneeled down in the rain to do honor to a dirty procession of monks which passed within his view, at a distance of some fifty or sixty yards. It is likely enough that, rooted in the woods of France and Norway, there were growing trees, when that sufferer was put to death, already marked by the Woodman, Fate, to come down and be sawn into boards, to make a certain movable frame-work with a sack and a knife in it, terrible in history. It is likely enough that in the rough outhouses of some tillers of the heavy lands adjacent to Paris, there were sheltered from the weather that very day, rule carts, bespattered with rustic mire, snuffed about by pigs, and roosted in by poultry, which the Farmer, Death, had already set apart to be his tumbrils of the Revolution. But, that Woodman and that Farmer, though they work unceasingly, work silently, and no one heard them as they went about with muffled tread: the rather, forasmuch as to entertain any suspicion that they were awake, was to be atheistical and traitorous.

In England, there was scarcely an amount of order and protection to justify much national boasting. Daring burglaries by armed men, and highway robberies, took place in the capital itself every night; families were publicly cautioned not to go out of town without removing their furniture to upholsterers' warehouses for security; the highwayman in the dark was a City tradesman in the light, and, being recognized and challenged by his fellow-tradesman whom he stopped in his character of "the Captain," gallantly shot him through the head and rode away; the mail was waylaid by seven robbers, and the guard shot three dead, and then got shot dead himself by the other four, "in consequence of the failure of his ammunition;" after which the mail was robbed in peace; that magnificent potentate, the Lord of London, was made to stand and deliver on Turnham Green, by one highwayman who despoiled the illustrious creature in sight of all his retinue; prisoners in London gaols fought battles with their turnkeys, and the majesty of the law fired blunderbusses in among them, loaded with rounds of shot and ball; thieves snipped off diamond crosses from the necks of noble lords at Court drawing-rooms; musketeers went into St. Giles's to search for contraband goods, and the mob fired on the musketeers, and the musketeers fired on the mob; and nobody thought any of these occurrences much out of the common way. In the midst of them, the hangman, ever busy and ever worse than useless, was in constant requisition. . . .

All these things, and a thousand like them, came to pass in and close upon the dear old year one thousand seven hundred and seventy-five. Environed by them, while the Woodman and the Farmer worked unheeded, those two of the large jaws, and those other two of the plain and the fair faces, trod with stir enough, and carried their divine rights with a high hand. Thus did the year one thousand seven hundred and seventy-five conduct their Greatness, and myriads of small creatures— the creatures of this chronicle among the rest—along the roads that lay before them.

CHARLES DICKENS
A Tale of Two Cities, 1859

You don't know about me without you have read a book by the name of *The Adventures of Tom Sawyer*; but that ain't no matter. That book was made by Mr. Mark Twain, and he told the truth, mainly. There was things which he stretched, but mainly he told the truth. That is nothing. I never seen anybody but lied one time or another, without it was Aunt Polly, or the widow, or maybe Mary. Aunt Polly —Tom's Aunt Polly, she is—and Mary, and the Widow Douglas is all told about in that book, which is mostly a true book, with some stretchers, as I said before.

Now the way that the book winds up is this: Tom and me found the money that the robbers hid in the cave, and it made us rich. We got six thousand dollars apiece—all gold. It was an awful sight of money when it was piled up. Well, Judge Thatcher he took it and put it out at interest, and it fetched us a dollar a day apiece all the year round— more than a body could tell what to do with. The Widow Douglas she took me for her son, and allowed she would sivilize me; but it was rough living in the house all the time, considering how dismal regular and decent the widow was in all her ways; and so when I couldn't stand it no longer I lit out. I got into my old rags and my sugar-hogshead again, and was free and satisfied. But Tom Sawyer he hunted me up and said he was going to start a band of robbers, and I might join if I would go back to the widow and be respectable. So I went back.

The widow she cried over me, and called me a poor lost lamb, and she called me a lot of other names, too, but she never meant no harm by it. She put me in them new clothes again, and I couldn't do nothing but sweat and sweat, and feel all cramped up. Well, then, the old thing commenced again. The widow rung a bell for supper, and you had to come to time. When you got to the table you couldn't go right to eating, but you had to wait for the widow to tuck down her head and grumble a little over the victuals, though there warn't really anything the matter with them,—that is, nothing, only everything was cooked by itself. In a barrel of odds and ends it is different; things get mixed up, and the juice kind of swaps around, and the things go better.

After supper she got out her book and learned me about Moses and the Bulrushers, and I was in a sweat to find out all about him; but by-and-by she let it out that Moses had been dead a considerable long time; so then I didn't care no more about him, because I don't take no stock in dead people.

Pretty soon I wanted to smoke, and asked the widow to let me. But she wouldn't. She said it was a mean practice and wasn't clean, and I must try to not do it any more. That is just the way with some people. They get down on a thing when they don't know nothing about it. Here she was a-bothering about Moses, which was no kin to her, and no use to anybody, being gone, you see, yet finding a power of fault with me for doing a thing that had some good in it. And she took snuff, too; of course that was all right, because she done it herself.

Her sister, Miss Watson, a tolerable slim old maid, with goggles on, had just come to live with her, and took a set at me now with a spelling-book. She worked me middling hard for about an hour, and then the widow made her ease up. I couldn't stood it much longer. Then for an hour it was deadly dull, and I was fidgety. Miss Watson would say, "Don't put your feet up there, Huckleberry;" and "Don't scrunch up like that, Huckleberry—set up straight;" and pretty soon she would say, "Don't gap and stretch like that, Huckleberry—why don't you try to behave?" Then she told me all about the bad place, and I said I wished I was there. She got mad then, but I didn't mean no harm. All I wanted was to go somewheres; all I wanted was a change, I warn't particular. She said it was wicked to say what I said; said she wouldn't say it for the whole world. . . .

Now she had got a start, and she went on and told me all about the good place. She said all a body would have to do there was to go around all day long with a harp and sing, for ever and ever. So I didn't think much of it. But I never said so. I asked her if she reckoned Tom Sawyer would go there, and she said not by a considerable sight. I was glad about that, because I wanted him and me to be together.

Miss Watson she kept pecking at me, and it got tiresome and lonesome. By-and-by they fetched the niggers in and had prayers, and then everybody was off to bed. I went up to my room with a piece of candle, and put it on the table. Then I set down in a chair by the window and tried to think of something cheerful, but it warn't no use. I felt so lonesome I most wished I was dead. The stars were shining, and the leaves rustled in the woods ever so mournful; and I heard an owl, away off, who-whooing about somebody that was dead, and a whippowill and a dog crying about somebody that was going to die; and the wind was trying to whisper something to me, and I couldn't make out what it was, and so it made the cold shivers run over me. Then away out in the woods I heard that kind of a sound that a ghost makes when it wants to tell about something that's on its mind and can't make itself understood, and so can't rest easy in its grave, and has to go about that way every night grieving. I got so down-hearted and scared I did wish I had some company. Pretty soon a spider went crawling up my shoulder, and I flipped it off and it lit in the candle; and before I could budge it was all shrivelled up. I didn't need anybody to tell me that that was an awful bad sign and would fetch me some bad luck, so I was scared and most shook the clothes off of me. I got up and turned around in my tracks three times and crossed my breast every time; and then I tied up a little lock of my hair with a thread to keep witches away. But I hadn't no confidence. You do that when you've lost a horseshoe that you've found, instead of nailing it up over the door, but I hadn't ever heard anybody say it was any way to keep off bad luck when you'd killed a spider.

I set down again, a-shaking all over, and got out my pipe for a smoke: for the house was all as still as death now, and so the widow wouldn't know. Well, after a long time I heard the clock away off in the town go boom—boom—boom—twelve licks; and all still again—stiller than ever. Pretty soon I heard a twig snap down in the dark amongst the trees—something was a stirring. I set still and listened. Directly I could just barely hear a *"me-yow! me-yow!"* down there. That was good! Says I, *"me-yow! me-yow!"* as soft as I could, and then I put out the light and scrambled out of the window on to the shed. Then I slipped down to the ground and crawled in among the trees, and, sure enough, there was Tom Sawyer waiting for me.

Mark Twain
The Adventures of Huckleberry Finn, 1885

Happy families are all alike; every unhappy family is unhappy in its own way.

Everything was in confusion in the Oblonskys' house. The wife had discovered that the husband was carrying on an intrigue with a French girl, who had been a governess in their family, and she had announced to her husband that she could not go on living in the same house with him. This position of affairs had now lasted three days, and not only the husband and wife themselves, but all the members of their family and household, were painfully conscious of it. Every person in the house felt that there was no sense in their living together, and that the stray people brought together by chance in any inn had more in common with one another than they, the members of the family and household of the Oblonskys. The wife did not leave her own room, the husband had not been at home for three days. The children ran wild all over the house; the English governess quarreled with the housekeeper, and wrote to a friend asking her to look out for a new situation for her; the man-cook had walked off the day before just at dinner-time; the kitchen-maid, and the coachman had given warning.

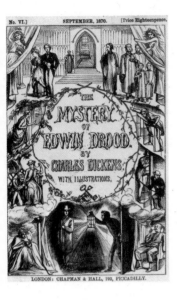

Three days after the quarrel, Prince Stepan Arkadyevitch Oblonsky —Stiva, as he was called in the fashionable world—woke up at his usual hour, that is, at eight o'clock in the morning, not in his wife's bedroom, but on the leather-covered sofa in his study. He turned over his stout, well-cared-for person on the springy sofa as though he would sink into a long sleep again; he vigorously embraced the pillow on the other side and buried his face in it; but all at once he jumped up, sat up on the sofa, and opened his eyes. . . .

. . . he cheerfully dropped his feet over the edge of the sofa, and felt about with them for his slippers, a present on his last birthday, worked for him by his wife on gold-colored morocco. And, as he had done every day for the last nine years, he stretched out his hand, without getting up, towards the place where his dressing-gown always hung in his bedroom. And thereupon he suddenly remembered that he was not sleeping in his wife's room, but in his study, and why: the smile vanished from his face, he knitted his brows.

"Ah, ah, ah! Oo! . . ." he muttered, recalling everything that had happened. And again every detail of his quarrel with his wife was present to his imagination, all the hopelessness of his position, and worst of all, his own fault.

Yes, she won't forgive me, and she can't forgive me. And the most awful thing about it is that it's all my fault—all my fault, though I'm not to blame. That's the point of the whole situation," he reflected. "Oh, oh, oh!" he kept repeating in despair, as he remembered the acutely painful sensations caused him by this quarrel.

Most unpleasant of all was the first minute when, on coming, happy and good-humored, from the theater, with a huge pear in his hand for his wife, he had not found his wife in the drawing-room, to his surprise had not found her in the study either, and saw her at last in her bedroom with the unlucky letter that revealed everything in her hand.

She, his Dolly, forever fussing and worrying over household details, and limited in her ideas, as he considered, was sitting perfectly still with the letter in her hand, looking at him with an expression of horror, despair, and indignation.

"What's this? this?" she asked, pointing to the letter.

And at this recollection, Stepan Arkadyevitch, as is so often the case, was not so much annoyed at the fact itself as at the way in which he had met his wife's words.

There happened to him at that instant what does happen to people when they are unexpectedly caught in something very disgraceful. He did not succeed in adapting his face to the position in which he was placed towards his wife by the discovery of his fault. Instead of being hurt, denying, defending himself, begging forgiveness, instead of remaining indifferent even—anything would have been better than what he did do—his face utterly involuntarily (reflex spinal action, reflected Stepan Arkadyevitch, who was fond of physiology)—utterly involuntarily assumed its habitual, good-humored, and therefore idiotic smile.

This idiotic smile he could not forgive himself. Catching sight of that smile, Dolly shuddered as though at physical pain, broke out with her characteristic heat into a flood of cruel words, and rushed out of the room. Since then she had refused to see her husband.

"It's that idiotic smile that's to blame for it all," thought Stepan Arkadyevitch.

"But what's to be done? What's to be done?" he said to himself in despair, and found no answer.

LEO TOLSTOY
Anna Karenina, 1873–77

The *Nellie*, a cruising yawl, swung to her anchor without a flutter of the sails, and was at rest. The flood had made, the wind was nearly calm, and being bound down the river, the only thing for it was to come to and wait for the turn of the tide.

The sea-reach of the Thames stretched before us like the beginning of an interminable waterway. In the offing the sea and the sky were welded together without a joint, and in the luminous space the tanned sails of the barges drifting up with the tide seemed to stand still in red clusters of canvas sharply peaked, with gleams of varnished spirits. A haze rested on the low shores that ran out to sea in vanishing flatness. The air was dark above Gravesend, and farther back still seemed condensed into a mournful gloom, brooding motionless over the biggest, and the greatest, town on earth.

The Director of Companies was our captain and our host. We four affectionately watched his back as he stood in the bows looking to seaward. On the whole river there was nothing that looked half so nautical. He resembled a pilot, which to a seaman is trustworthiness personi-fied. It was difficult to realize his work was not out there in the lumi-nous estuary, but behind him, within the brooding gloom.

Between us there was, as I have already said somewhere, the bond of the sea. Besides holding our hearts together through long periods of separation, it had the effect of making us tolerant of each other's yarns —and even convictions. The lawyer—the best of old fellows—had, because of his many years and many virtues, the only cushion on deck, and was lying on the only rug. The accountant had brought out already a box of dominoes, and was toying architecturally with the bones. Marlow sat cross-legged right aft, leaning against the mizzen-mast. He had sunken cheeks, a yellow complexion, a straight back, an ascetic aspect, and, with his arms dropped, the palms of hands outwards, resembled an idol. The director, satisfied the anchor had good hold, made his way aft and sat down amongst us. We exchanged a few words lazily. Afterwards there was silence on board the yacht. For some reason or other we did not begin that game of dominoes. We felt medi-tative, and fit for nothing but placid staring. The day was ending in a serenity of still and exquisite brilliance. The water shone pacifically; the sky, without a speck, was a benign immensity of unstained light; the very mist on the Essex marshes was like a gauzy and radiant fabric, hung from the wooded rises inland, and draping the low shores in dia-phanous folds. Only the gloom to the west, brooding over the upper reaches, became more somber every minute, as if angered by the approach of the sun.

And at last, in its curved and imperceptible fall, the sun sank low, and from glowing white changed to a dull red without rays and with-out heat, as if about to go out suddenly, stricken to death by the touch of that gloom brooding over a crowd of men.

Forthwith a change came over the waters, and the serenity became less brilliant but more profound. The old river in its broad reach rested unruffled at the decline of day, after ages of good service done to the race that peopled its banks, spread out in the tranquil dignity of a waterway leading to the uttermost ends of the earth. We looked at the venerable stream not in the vivid flush of a short day that comes and departs forever, but in the august light of abiding memories. And indeed nothing is easier for man who has, as the phrase goes, "followed the sea" with reverence and affection, than to evoke the great spirit of the past upon the lower reaches of the Thames. The tidal current runs to and fro in its unceasing service, crowded with memories of men and ships it had borne to the rest of home or to the battles of the sea. It had known and served all the men of whom the nation is proud, from Sir Francis Drake to Sir John Franklin, knights all, titled and untitled —the great knights-errant of the sea. It had borne all the ships whose names are like jewels flashing in the night of time, from the *Golden Hind* returning with her round flanks full of treasure, to be visited by the Queen's Highness and thus pass out of the gigantic tale, to the

Erebus and *Terror*, bound on other conquests—and that never returned. It had known the ships and the men. They had sailed from Deptford, from Greenwich, from Erith—the adventurers and the settlers; kings' ships and the ships of men on 'Change captains, admirals, the dark "interlopers" of the Eastern trade, and the commissioned "generals" of East India fleets. Hunters for gold or pursuers of fame, they all had gone out on that stream, bearing the sword, and often the torch, messengers of the might within the land, bearers of a spark from the sacred fire. What greatness had not floated on the ebb of that river into the mystery of an unknown earth! . . . The dreams of men, the seed of commonwealths, the germs of empires.

The sun set; the dusk fell on the stream, and light began to appear along the shore. The Chapman light house, a three-legged thing erect on a mud-flat, shone strongly. Lights of ships moved in the fairway—a great stir of lights going up and going down. And farther west on the upper reaches the place of the monstrous town was still marked ominously on the sky, a brooding gloom in sunshine, a lurid glare under the stars.

"And this also," said Marlow suddenly, "has been one of the dark places of the earth."

JOSEPH CONRAD
Heart of Darkness, 1902

U nder certain circumstances there are few hours in life more agreeable than the hour dedicated to the ceremony known as afternoon tea. There are circumstances in which, whether you partake of the tea or not—some people of course never do,—the situation is in itself delightful. Those that I have in mind in beginning to unfold this simple history offered an admirable setting to an innocent pastime. The implements of the little feast had been disposed upon the lawn of an old English country-house, in what I should call the perfect middle of a splendid summer afternoon. Part of the afternoon had waned, but much of it was left, and what was left was of the finest and rarest quality. Real dusk would not arrive for many hours; but the flood of summer light had begun to ebb, the air had grown mellow, the shadows were long upon the smooth, dense turf. They lengthened slowly, however, and the scene expressed that sense of leisure still to come which is perhaps the chief source of one's enjoyment of such a scene at such an hour. From five o'clock to eight is on certain occasions a little eternity; but on such an occasion as this the interval could be only an eternity of pleasure. The persons concerned in it were taking their pleasure quietly, and they were not of the sex which is supposed to furnish the regular votaries of the ceremony I have mentioned. The shadows on the perfect lawn were straight and angular; they were the shadows of an old man sitting in a deep wicker-chair near the low table on which the tea had been served, and of two younger men strolling to and fro, in desultory talk, in front of him. The old man had his cup in his hand; it was an unusually large cup, of a different pattern from the rest of the set and painted in brilliant colours. He disposed of its contents with much circumspection, holding it for a long time close to his chin, with his face turned to the house. His companions had either finished their tea or were indifferent to their privilege; they smoked cigarettes as they continued to stroll. One of them, from time to time, as he passed, looked with a certain attention at the elder man, who, unconscious of observation, rested his eyes upon the rich red front of his dwelling. The house that rose beyond the lawn was a structure to repay such consideration. . . .

The old gentleman at the tea-table, who had come from America thirty years before, had brought with him, at the top of his baggage, his American physiognomy; and he had not only brought it with him, but he had kept it in the best order, so that, if necessary, he might have taken it back to his own country with perfect confidence. At present, obviously, nevertheless, he was not likely to displace himself; his journeys were over and he was taking the rest that precedes the great rest. He had a narrow, clean-shaven face, with features evenly distributed and an expression of placid acuteness. It was evidently a face in which the range of representation was not large, so that the air of contented shrewdness was all the more of a merit. It seemed to tell that he had been successful in life, yet it seemed to tell also that his success had not been exclusive and invidious, but had had much of the inoffensiveness of failure. He had certainly had a great experience of men, but there was an almost rustic simplicity in the faint smile that played upon his lean, spacious cheek and lighted up his humorous eye as he at last slowly and carefully deposited his big tea-cup upon the table. He was neatly dressed, in well-brushed black; but a shawl was folded upon his knees, and his feet were encased in thick, embroidered slippers. A beautiful collie dog lay upon the grass near his chair, watching the master's face almost as tenderly as the master took in the still more magisterial physiognomy of the house; and a little bristling, bustling terrier bestowed a desultory attendance upon the other gentlemen.

One of these was a remarkably well-made man of five-and-thirty, with a face as English as that of the old gentleman I have just sketched was something else; a noticeably handsome face, fresh-coloured, fair and frank, with firm, straight features, a lively grey eye and the rich adornment of a chestnut beard. This person had a certain fortunate, brilliant exceptional look—the air of a happy temperament fertilised by a high civilisation—which would have made almost any observer envy him at a venture. He was booted and spurred, as if he had dismounted from a long ride; he wore a white hat, which looked too large for him; he held his two hands behind him, and in one of them—a large, white, well-shaped fist—was crumpled a pair of soiled dog-skin gloves.

HENRY JAMES
The Portrait of a Lady, 1881

The Brangwens had lived for generations on the Marsh Farm, in the meadows where the Erewash twisted sluggishly through alder trees, separating Derbyshire from Nottinghamshire. Two miles away, a church-tower stood on a hill, the houses of the little country town climbing assiduously up to it. Whenever one of the Brangwens in the fields lifted his head from his work, he saw the church-tower at Ilkeston in the empty sky. So that as he turned again to the horizontal land, he was aware of something standing above him and beyond him in the distance.

There was a look in the eyes of the Brangwens as if they were expecting something unknown, about which they were eager. They had that air of readiness for what would come to them, a kind of surety, an expectancy, the look of an inheritor.

They were fresh, blond, slow-speaking people, revealing themselves plainly, but slowly, so that one could watch the change in their eyes from laughter to anger, blue, lit-up laughter, to a hard blue-staring anger; through all the irresolute stages of the sky when the weather is changing.

Living on rich land, on their own land, near to a growing town, they had forgotten what it was to be in straitened circumstances. They had never become rich, because there were always children, and the patrimony was divided every time. But always, at the Marsh, there was ample.

So the Brangwens came and went without fear of necessity, working hard because of the life that was in them, not for want of the money. Neither were they thriftless. They were aware of the last halfpenny, and instinct made them not waste the peeling of their apple, for it would help to feed the cattle. But heaven and earth was teeming around them, and how should this cease? They felt the rush of the sap in spring, they knew the wave which cannot halt, but every year throws forward the seed to begetting, and, falling back, leaves the young-born on the earth. They knew the intercourse between heaven and earth, sunshine drawn into the breast and bowels, the rain sucked up in the daytime, nakedness that comes under the wind in autumn, showing the birds' nests no longer worth hiding. Their life and interrelations were such; feeling the pulse and body of the soil, that opened to their furrow for the grain, and became smooth and supple after their ploughing, and clung to their feet with a weight that pulled like desire, lying hard and unresponsive when the crops were to be shorn away. The young corn waved and was silken, and the lustre slid along the limbs of the men who saw it. They took the udder of the cows, the cows yielded milk and pulse against the hands of the men, the pulse of the blood of the teats of the cows beat into the pulse of the hands of the men. They mounted their horses, and held life between the grip of their knees, they harnessed their horses at the wagon, and, with hand on the bridle-rings, drew the heaving of the horses after their will.

In autumn the partridges whirred up, birds in flocks blew like spray across the fallow, rooks appeared on the grey, watery heavens, and flew cawing into the winter. Then the men sat by the fire in the house where the women moved about with surety, and the limbs and the body of the men were impregnated with the day, cattle and earth and vegetation and the sky, the men sat by the fire and their brains were inert, as their blood flowed heavy with the accumulation from the living day.

The women were different. On them too was the drowse of blood-intimacy, calves sucking and hens running together in droves, and young geese palpitating in the hand while the food was pushed down their throttle. But the women looked out from the heated, blind intercourse of farm-life, to the spoken world beyond. They were aware of the lips and the mind of the world speaking and giving utterance, they heard the sound in the distance, and they strained to listen.

It was enough for the men, that the earth heaved and opened its furrow to them, that the wind blew to dry the wet wheat, and set the young ears of corn wheeling freshly round about; it was enough that they helped the cow in labour, or ferreted the rats from under the barn, or broke the back of a rabbit with a sharp knock of the hand. So much warmth and generating and pain and death did they know in their blood, earth and sky and beast and green plants, so much exchange and interchange they had with these, that they lived full and surcharged, their senses full fed, their faces always turned to the heat of the blood, staring into the sun, dazed with looking towards the source of generation, unable to turn round.

But the woman wanted another form of life than this, something that was not blood-intimacy. Her house faced out from the farm-buildings and fields, looked out to the road and the village with church and Hall and the world beyond. She stood to see the far-off world of cities and governments and the active scope of man, the magic land to her, where secrets were made known and desires fulfilled. She faced outwards to where men moved dominant and creative, having turned their back on the pulsing heat of creation, and with this behind them, were set out to discover what was beyond, to enlarge their own scope and range and freedom; whereas the Brangwen men faced inwards to the teeming life of creation, which poured unresolved into their veins.

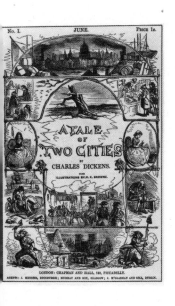

Looking out, as she must, from the front of her house towards the activity of man in the world at large, whilst her husband looked out to the back at sky and harvest and beast and land, she strained her eyes to see what man had done in fighting outwards to knowledge, she strained to hear how he uttered himself in his conquest, her deepest desire hung on the battle that she heard, far off, being waged on the edge of the unknown. She also wanted to know, and to be of the fighting host.

At home, even so near as Cossethay, was the vicar, who spoke the other, magic language, and had the other, finer bearing, both of which she could perceive, but could never attain to. The vicar moved in worlds beyond where her own menfolk existed. Did she not know her own menfolk: fresh, slow, full-built men, masterful enough, but easy, native to the earth, lacking outwardness and range of motion. Whereas the vicar, dark and dry and small beside her husband, had yet a quickness and a range of being that made Brangwen, in his large geniality, seem dull and local. She knew her husband. But in the vicar's nature was that which passed beyond her knowledge. As Brangwen had power over the cattle so the vicar had power over her husband. What was it in the vicar, that raised him above the common men as man is raised above the beast? She craved to know. She craved to achieve this higher being, if not in herself, then in her children. That which makes a man strong even if he be little and frail in body, just as any man is little and frail beside a bull, and yet stronger than the bull, what was it? It was not money nor power nor position. What power had the vicar over Tom Brangwen—none. Yet strip them and set them on a desert island, and the vicar was the master. His soul was master of the other man's. And why—why? She decided it was a question of knowledge.

D.H. LAWRENCE
The Rainbow, 1915

Once upon a time and a very good time it was there was a moocow coming down along the road and this moocow that was down along the road met a nicens little boy named baby tuckoo. . . .

His father told him that story: his father looked at him through a glass: he had a hairy face.

He was baby tuckoo. The moocow came down the road where Betty Byrne lived: she sold lemon platt.

> *O, the wild rose blossoms*
> *On the little green place.*

He sang that song. That was his song.

> *O, the green wothe botheth.*

When you wet the bed, first it is warm then it gets cold. His mother put on the oilsheet. That had the queer smell.

His mother had a nicer smell than his father. She played on the piano the sailor's hornpipe for him to dance. He danced:

> *Tralala lala,*
> *Tralala tralaladdy,*
> *Tralala lala,*
> *Tralala lala.*

Uncle Charles and Dante clapped. They were older than his father and mother but Uncle Charles was older than Dante.

Dante had two brushes in her press. The brush with the maroon velvet back was for Michael Davitt and the brush with the green velvet back was for Parnell. Dante gave him a cachou every time he brought her a piece of tissue paper. . . .

The wide playgrounds were swarming with boys. All were shouting and the prefects urged them on with strong cries. The evening air was pale and chilly and after every charge and thud of the foot-ballers the greasy leather orb flew like a heavy bird through the grey light. He kept on the fringe of his line, out of sight of his prefect, out of the reach of the rude feet, feigning to run now and then. He felt his body small and weak amid the throng of players and his eyes were weak and watery. Rody Kickham was not like that: he would be captain of the third line all the fellows said.

Rody Kickham was a decent fellow but Nasty Roche was a stink. Rody Kickham had greaves in his number and a hamper in the refectory. Nasty Roche had big hands. He called the Friday pudding dog-in-the-blanket. And one day he had asked:

—What is your name?

Stephen had answered: Stephen Dedalus.

Then Nasty Roche had said:

—What kind of a name is that?

And when Stephen had not been able to answer Nasty Roche had asked:

—What is your father?

Stephen had answered:

—A gentleman.

Then Nasty Roche had asked:

—Is he a magistrate?

He crept about from point to point on the fringe of his line, making little runs now and then. But his hands were bluish with cold. He kept his hands in the side pockets of his belted grey suit. That was a belt round his pocket. And belt was also to give a fellow a belt. One day a fellow had said to Cantwell:

—I'd give you such a belt in a second.

Cantwell had answered:

—Go and fight your match. Give Cecil Thunder a belt. I'd like to see you. He'd give you a toe in the rump for yourself.

That was not a nice expression. His mother had told him not to speak with the rough boys in the college. Nice mother! The first day in the hall of the castle when she had said goodbye she had put up her veil double to her nose to kiss him: and her nose and eyes were red. But he had pretended not to see that she was going to cry. She was a nice mother but she was not so nice when she cried. And his father had given him two five-shilling pieces for pocket money. And his father had told him if he wanted anything to write home to him and, whatever he did, never to peach on a fellow. Then at the door of the castle the rector had shaken hands with his father and mother, his soutane fluttering in the breeze, and the car had driven off with his father and mother on it. They had cried to him from the car, waving their hands:

—Good-bye, Stephen, goodbye!

—Good-bye, Stephen, goodbye!

JAMES JOYCE

A Portrait of the Artist as a Young Man, 1916

For a long time I used to go to bed early. Sometimes, when I had put out my candle, my eyes would close so quickly that I had not even time to say "I'm going to sleep." And half an hour later the thought that it was time to go to sleep would awaken me; I would try to put away the book which, I imagined, was still in my hands, and to blow out the light; I had been thinking all the time, while I was asleep, of what I had just been reading, but my thoughts had run into a channel of their own, until myself seemed actually to have become the subject of my book: a church, a quartet, the rivalry between François I and Charles V. This impression would persist for some moments after I was awake; it did not disturb my mind, but it lay like scales upon my eyes and prevented them from registering the fact that the candle was no longer burning. Then it would begin to seem unintelligible, as the thoughts of a former existence must be to a reincarnate spirit; the subject of my book would separate itself from me, leaving me free to choose whether I would form part of it or no; and at the same time my sight would return and I would be astonished to find myself in a state of darkness, pleasant and restful enough for the eyes, and even more, perhaps, for my mind, to which it appeared incomprehensible, without a cause, a matter dark indeed. . . .

I would lay my cheeks gently against the comfortable cheeks of my pillow, as plump and blooming as the cheeks of babyhood. Or I would strike a match to look at my watch. Nearly midnight. The hour when an invalid, who has been obliged to start on a journey and to sleep in a strange hotel, awakens in a moment of illness and sees with glad relief a streak of daylight shewing under his bedroom door. Oh, joy of joys! it is morning. The servants will be about in a minute: he can ring, and some one will come to look after him. The thought of being made comfortable gives him strength to endure his pain. He is certain he heard footsteps: they come nearer, and then die away. The ray of light beneath his door is extinguished. It is midnight; some one has turned out the gas; the last servant has gone to bed, and he must lie all night in agony with no one to bring him any help.

I would fall asleep, and often I would be awake again for short snatches only, just long enough to hear the regular creaking of the wainscot, or to open my eyes to settle the shifting kaleidoscope of the darkness, to savour, in an instantaneous flash of perception, the sleep which lay heavy upon the furniture, the room, the whole surroundings of which I formed but an insignificant part and whose unconsciousness I should very soon return to share. Or, perhaps, while I was asleep I had returned without the least effort to an earlier stage in my life, now for ever outgrown; and had come under the thrall of one of my childish terrors, such as that old terror of my great-uncle's pulling my curls, which was effectually dispelled on the day—the dawn of a new era to me—on which they were finally cropped from my head. I had forgotten that event during my sleep; I remembered it again immediately I had succeeded in making myself wake up to escape my great-

uncle's fingers; still, as a measure of precaution, I would bury the whole of my head in the pillow before returning to the world of dreams. . . .

Many years had elapsed during which nothing of Combray, save what was comprised in the theatre and the drama of my going to bed there, had any existence for me, when one day in winter, as I came home, my mother, seeing that I was cold, offered me some tea, a thing I did not ordinarily take. I declined at first, and then, for no particular reason, changed my mind. She sent out for one of those short, plump little cakes called 'petites madeleines,' which look as though they had been moulded in the fluted scallop of a pilgrim's shell. And soon, mechanically, weary after a dull day with the prospect of a depressing morrow, I raised to my lips a spoonful of the tea in which I had soaked a morsel of the cake. No sooner had the warm liquid, and the crumbs with it, touched my palate than a shudder ran through my whole body, and I stopped, intent upon the extraordinary changes that were taking place. An exquisite pleasure had invaded my senses, but individual, detached, with no suggestion of its origin. And at once the vicissitudes of life had become indifferent to me, its disasters innocuous, its brevity illusory—this new sensation having had on me the effect which love has of filling me with a precious essence; or rather this essence was not in me, it was myself. I had ceased now to feel mediocre, accidental, mortal. Whence could it have come to me, this all-powerful joy? I was conscious that it was connected with the taste of tea and cake, but that it infinitely transcended those savours, could not, indeed, be of the same nature as theirs. Whence did it come? What did it signify? How could I seize upon and define it?

I drink a second mouthful, in which I find nothing more than in the first, a third, which gives me rather less than the second. It is time to stop; the potion is losing its magic. It is plain that the object of my quest, the truth, lies not in the cup but in myself. The tea has called up in me, but does not itself understand, and can only repeat indefinitely with a gradual loss of strength, the same testimony; which I, too, cannot interpret, though I hope at least to be able to call upon the tea for it again and to find it there presently, intact and at my disposal, for my final enlightenment. I put down my cup and examine my own mind. It is for it to discover the truth. But how? What an abyss of uncertainty whenever the mind feels that some part of it has strayed beyond its own borders; when it, the seeker, is at once the dark region through which it must go seeking, where all its equipment will avail it nothing. Seek? More than that: create. It is face to face with something which does not so far exist, to which it alone can give reality and substance, which it alone can bring into the light of day.

And I begin again to ask myself what it could have been, this unremembered state which brought with it no logical proof of its existence, but only the sense that it was a happy, that it was a real state in whose presence other states of consciousness melted and vanished. I decided to attempt to make it reappear. I retrace my thoughts to the moment at which I drank the first spoonful of tea. I find again the same state. . . .

And suddenly the memory returns. The taste was that of the little crumb of madeleine which on Sunday mornings at Combray (because on those mornings I did not go out before church-time), when I went to say good day to her in her bedroom, my aunt Léonie used to give me, dipping it first in her own cup of real or of lime-flower tea. The sight of the little madeleine had recalled nothing to my mind before I tasted it; perhaps because I had so often seen such things in the interval, without tasting them, on the trays in pastry-cook's windows, that their image had dissociated itself from those Combray days to take its place among others more recent; perhaps because of those memories, so long abandoned and put out of mind, nothing now survived, everything was scattered; the forms of things, including that of the little scallop-shell of pastry, so richly sensual under its severe, religious folds, were either obliterated or had been so long dormant as to have lost the power of expansion which would have allowed them to resume their place in my consciousness. But when from a long-distant past nothing subsists, after the people are dead, after the things are broken and scattered, still alone, more fragile, but with more vitality, more unsubstantial, more persistent, more faithful, the smell and taste of things remain poised a long time, like souls, ready to remind us, waiting and hoping for their moment, amid the ruins of all the rest; and bear unfaltering, in the tiny and almost impalpable drop of their essence, the vast structure of recollection.

And once I had recognized the taste of the crumb of madeleine soaked in her decoction of lime-flowers which my aunt used to give me (although I did not yet know and must long postpone the discovery of why this memory made me so happy) immediately the old grey house upon the street, where her room was, rose up like the scenery of a theatre to attach itself to the little pavilion, opening on to the garden, which had been built out behind it for my parents (the isolated panel which until that moment had been all that I could see); and with the house the town, from morning to night and in all weathers, the Square where I was sent before luncheon, the streets along which I used to run errands, the country roads we took when it was fine. And just as the Japanese amuse themselves by filling a porcelain bowl with water and steeping in it little crumbs of paper which until then are without character or form, but, the moment they become wet, stretch themselves and bend, take on colour and distinctive shape, become flowers or houses or people, permanent and recognisable, so in that moment all the flowers in our garden and in M. Swann's park, and the water-lilies on the Vivonne and the good folk of the village and their little dwellings and the parish church and the whole of Combray and of its surroundings, taking their proper shapes and growing solid, sprang into being, town and gardens alike, from my cup of tea.

Marcel Proust
Remembrance of Things Past, 1913–27

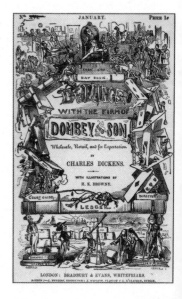

In the late summer of that year we lived in a house in a village that looked across the river and the plain to the mountains. In the bed of the river there were pebbles and boulders, dry and white in the sun, and the water was clear and swiftly moving and blue in the channels. Troops went by the house and down the road and the dust they raised powdered the leaves of the trees. The trunks of the trees too were dusty and the leaves fell early that year and we saw the troops marching along the road and the dust rising and leaves, stirred by the breeze, falling and the soldiers marching and afterward the road bare and white except for the leaves.

The plain was rich with crops; there were many orchards of fruit trees and beyond the plain the mountains were brown and bare. There was fighting in the mountains and at night we could see the flashes from the artillery. In the dark it was like summer lightning, but the nights were cool and there was not the feeling of a storm coming.

Sometimes in the dark we heard the troops marching under the window and guns going past pulled by motor-tractors. There was much traffic at night and many mules on the roads with boxes of ammunition on each side of their pack-saddles and gray motor-trucks that carried men, and other trucks with loads covered with canvas that moved slower in the traffic. There were big guns too that passed in the day drawn by tractors, the long barrels of the guns covered with green branches and green leafy branches and vines laid over the tractors. To the north we could look across a valley and see a forest of chestnut trees and behind it another mountain on this side of the river. There was fighting for that mountain too, but it was not successful, and in the fall when the rains came the leaves all fell from the chestnut trees and the branches were bare and the trunks black with rain. The vineyards were thin and bare-branched too and all the country wet and brown and dead with the autumn. There were mists over the river and clouds on the mountain and the trucks splashed mud on the road and the troops were muddy and wet in their capes; their rifles were wet and under their capes the two leather cartridge-boxes . . . bulged. . . .

There were small gray motor-cars that passed going very fast; usually there was an officer on the seat with the driver and more officers in the back seat. They splashed more mud than the camions even and if one of the officers in the back was very small and sitting between two generals, he himself so small that you could not see his face but only the top of his cap and his narrow back, and if the car went especially fast it was probably the King. He lived in Udine and came out in this way nearly every day to see how things were going, and things went very badly.

At the start of the winter came the permanent rain and with the rain came the cholera. But it was checked and in the end only seven thousand died of it in the army.

ERNEST HEMINGWAY
A Farewell to Arms, 1929

On the pleasant shore of the French Riviera, about half way between Marseilles and the Italian border, stands a large, proud, rose-colored hotel. Deferential palms cool its flushed façade, and before it stretches a short dazzling beach. Lately it has become a summer resort of notable and fashionable people; a decade ago it was almost deserted after its English clientele went north in April. Now, many bungalows cluster near it, but when this story begins only the cupolas of a dozen old villas rotted like water lilies among the massed pines between Gausse's Hôtel des Etrangers and Cannes, five miles away.

The hotel and its bright tan prayer rug of a beach were one. In the early morning the distant image of Cannes, the pink and cream of old fortifications, the purple Alp that bounded Italy, were cast across the water and lay quavering in the ripples and rings sent up by sea-plants through the clear shallows. Before eight a man came down to the beach in a blue bathrobe and with much preliminary application to his person of the chilly water, and much grunting and loud breathing, floundered a minute in the sea. When he had gone, beach and bay were quiet for an hour. Merchantmen crawled westward on the horizon; bus boys shouted in the hotel court; the dew dried upon the pines. In another hour the horns of motors began to blow down from the winding road along the low range of the Maures, which separates the littoral from true Provençal France.

A mile from the sea, where pines give way to dusty poplars, is an isolated railroad stop, whence one June morning in 1925 a victoria brought a woman and her daughter down to Gausse's Hotel. The mother's face was of a fading prettiness that would soon be patted with broken veins; her expression was both tranquil and aware in a pleasant way. However, one's eyes moved on quickly to her daughter, who had magic in her pink palms and her cheeks lit to a lovely flame, like the thrilling flush of children after their cold baths in the evening. Her fine high forehead sloped gently up to where her hair, bordering it like an armorial shield, burst into lovelocks and waves and curlicues of ash blonde and gold. Her eyes were bright, big, clear, wet, and shining, the color of her cheeks was real, breaking close to the surface from the strong young pump of her heart. Her body hovered delicately on the last edge of childhood—she was almost eighteen, nearly complete, but the dew was still on her. . . .

At the hotel the girl made the reservation in idiomatic but rather flat French, like something remembered. When they were installed on the ground floor she walked into the glare of the French windows and out a few steps onto the stone veranda that ran the length of the hotel. When she walked she carried herself like a ballet-dancer, not slumped down on her hips but held up in the small of her back. Out there the hot light clipped close her shadow and she retreated—it was too bright to see. Fifty yards away the Mediterranean yielded up its pigments, moment by moment, to the brutal sunshine; below the balustrade a faded Buick cooked on the hotel drive.

Indeed, of all the region only the beach stirred with activity. Three British nannies sat knitting the slow pattern of Victorian England, the pattern of the forties, the sixties, and the eighties, into sweaters and socks, to the tune of gossip as formalized as incantation; closer to the sea a dozen persons kept house under striped umbrellas, while their dozen children pursued unintimidated fish through the shallows or lay naked and glistening with cocoanut oil out in the sun.

F. Scott Fitzgerald
Tender Is the Night, 1934

From a little after two o'clock until almost sundown of the long still hot weary dead September afternoon they sat in what Miss Coldfield still called the office because her father had called it that—a dim hot airless room with the blinds all closed and fastened for forty-three summers because when she was a girl someone had believed that light and moving air carried heat and that dark was always cooler, and which (as the sun shone fuller and fuller on that side of the house) became latticed with yellow slashes full of dust motes which Quentin thought of as being flecks of the dead old dried paint itself blown inward from the scaling blinds as wind might have blown them. There was a wistaria vine blooming for the second time that summer on a wooden trellis before one window, into which sparrows came now and then in random gusts, making a dry vivid dusty sound before going away: and opposite Quentin, Miss Coldfield in the eternal black which she had worn for forty-three years now, whether for sister, father, or nothusband none knew, sitting so bolt upright in the straight hard chair that was so tall for her that her legs hung straight and rigid as if she had iron shinbones and ankles, clear of the floor with that air of impotent and static rage like children's feet, and talking in that grim haggard amazed voice until at last listening would renege and hearing-sense self-confound and the long-dead object of her impotent yet indomitable frustration would appear, as though outraged recapitulation evoked, quiet inattentive and harmless, out of the biding and dreamy and victorious dust.

Her voice would not cease, it would just vanish. There would be the dim coffin-smelling gloom sweet and oversweet with the twice-bloomed wistaria against the outer wall by the savage quiet September sun impacted distilled and hyperdistilled, into which came now and then the loud cloudy flutter of the sparrows like a flat limber stick whipped by an idle boy, and the rank smell of female old flesh long embattled in virginity while the wan haggard face watched him above the faint triangle of lace at wrists and throat from the too tall chair in which she resembled a crucified child and the voice not ceasing but vanishing into and then out of the long intervals like a stream, a trickle running from patch to patch of dried sand, and the ghost mused with shadowy docility as if it were the voice which he haunted where a more fortunate one would have had a house. Out of quiet thunderclap he would abrupt (man-horse-demon) upon a scene peaceful and decorous as a schoolprize water color faint sulphur-reek still in hair clothes and beard, with grouped behind him his band of wild niggers like beasts half tamed to walk upright like men, in attitudes wild and reposed, and manacled among them the French architect with his air grim, haggard, and tatter-ran. Immobile, bearded and hand palm-lifted the horseman sat; behind him the wild black and the captive architect huddled quietly, carrying in bloodless paradox the shovels and picks and axes of peaceful conquest. Then in the long unamaze Quentin seemed to watch them overrun suddenly the hundred square miles of tranquil and astonished earth and drag house and formal gardens violently out of the soundless Nothing and clap them down like cards upon a table beneath the up-palm immobile and pontific, creating the Sutpen's Hundred, the *Be Sutpen's Hundred* like the oldentime *Be Light*. Then hearing would reconcile and he would seem to listen to two separate Quentins now—the Quentin Compson preparing for Harvard in the South, the deep South dead since 1865 and peopled with garrulous outraged baffled ghosts, listening, having to listen, to one of the ghosts which had refused to lie still even longer than most had, telling him about old ghost-times; and the Quentin Compson who was still too young to deserve yet to be a ghost, but nevertheless having to be one for all that, since he was born and bred in the deep South the same as she was—the two separate Quentins now talking to one another in the long silence of notpeople, in notlanguage, like this: *It seems that this demon—his name was Sutpen—(Colonel Sutpen)—Colonel Sutpen. Who came out of nowhere and without warning upon the land with a band of strange niggers and built a plantation—(Tore violently a plantation, Miss Rosa Coldfield says)—tore violently. And married her sister Ellen and begot a son and a daughter which—(Without gentleness begot, Miss Rosa Coldfield says)—without gentleness. Which should have been the jewels of his pride and the shield and comfort of his old age, only—(Only they destroyed him or something or he destroyed them or something. And died)—and died. Without regret, Miss Rosa Coldfield says—(Save by her) Yes, save by her. (And by Quentin Compson) Yes. And by Quentin Compson.*

WILLIAM FAULKNER
Absalom, Absalom! 1936

To the red country and part of the gray country of Oklahoma, the last rains came gently, and they did not cut the scarred earth. The plows crossed and recrossed the rivulet marks. The last rains lifted the corn quickly and scattered weed colonies and grass along the sides of the roads so that the gray country and the dark red country began to disappear under a green cover. In the last part of May the sky grew pale and the clouds that had hung in high puffs for so long in the spring were dissipated. The sun flared down on the growing corn day after day until a line of brown spread along the edge of each green bayonet. The clouds appeared, and went away, and in a while they did not try any more. The weeds grew darker green to protect themselves, and they did not spread any more. The surface of the earth crusted, a thin hard crust, and as the sky became pale, so the earth became pale, pink in the red country and white in the gray country.

In the water-cut gullies the earth dusted down in dry little streams. Gophers and ant lions started small avalanches. And as the sharp sun struck day after day, the leaves of the young corn became less stiff and erect; they bent in a curve at first, and then, as the central ribs of strength grew weak, each leaf tilted downward. Then it was June, and the sun shone more fiercely. The brown lines on the corn leaves widened and moved in on the central ribs. The weeds frayed and edged back toward their roots. The air was thin and the sky more pale; and every day the earth paled.

In the roads where the teams moved, where the wheels milled the ground and the hooves of the horses beat the ground, the dirt crust broke and the dust formed. Every moving thing lifted the dust into the air: a walking man lifted a thin layer as high as his waist, and a wagon lifted the dust as high as the fence tops, and an automobile boiled a cloud behind it. The dust was long in settling back again.

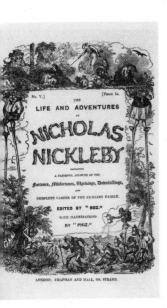

When June was half gone, the big clouds moved up out of Texas and the Gulf, high heavy clouds, rain-heads. The men in the fields looked up at the clouds and sniffed at them and held wet fingers up to sense the wind. And the horses were nervous while the clouds were up. The rain-heads dropped a little spattering and hurried on to some other country. Behind them the sky was pale again and the sun flared. In the dust there were drop craters where the rain had fallen, and there were clean splashes on the corn, and that was all. . . .

The wind grew stronger, whisked under stones, carried up straws and old leaves, and even little clods, marking its course as it sailed across the fields. The air and the sky darkened and through them the sun shone redly, and there was a raw sting in the air. During a night the wind raced faster over the land, dug cunningly among the rootlets of the corn, and the corn fought the wind with its weakened leaves until the roots were freed by the prying wind and then each stalk settled wearily sideways toward the earth and pointed the direction of the wind.

The dawn came, but no day. In the gray sky a red sun appeared, a dim red circle that gave a little light, like dusk; and as that day advanced, the dusk slipped back toward darkness, and the wind cried and whimpered over the fallen corn.

Men and women huddled in their houses, and they tied handkerchiefs over their noses when they went out, and wore goggles to protect their eyes.

When the night came again it was black night, for the stars could not pierce the dust to get down, and the window lights could not even spread beyond their own yards. Now the dust was evenly mixed with the air, an emulsion of dust and air. Houses were shut tight, and cloth wedged around doors and windows, but the dust came in so thinly that it could not be seen in the air, and it settled like pollen on the chairs and tables; on the dishes. The people brushed it from their shoulders. Little lines of dust lay at the door sills.

In the middle of that night the wind passed on and left the land quiet. The dust-filled air muffled sound more completely than fog does. The people, lying in their beds, heard the wind stop. They awakened when the rushing wind was gone. They lay quietly and listened deep into the stillness. Then the roosters crowed, and their voices were muffled, and the people stirred restlessly in their beds and wanted the morning. They knew it would take a long time for the dust to settle out of the air. In the morning the dust hung like fog, and the sun was as red as ripe new blood. All day the dust sifted down from the sky, and the next day it sifted down. An even blanket covered the earth. It settled on the corn, piled up on the tops of the fence posts, piled up on the wires; it settled on roofs, blanketed the weeds and trees.

The people came out of their houses and smelled the hot stinging air and covered their noses from it. And the children came out of the houses, but they did not run or shout as they would have done after a rain. Men stood by their fences and looked at the ruined corn, drying fast now, only a little green showing through the film of dust. The men were silent and they did not move often. And the women came out of the houses to stand beside their men—to feel whether this time the men would break. The women studied the men's faces secretly, for the corn could go, as long as something else remained. The children stood near by, drawing figures in the dust with bare toes, and the children sent exploring senses out to see whether men and women would break. The children peeked at the faces of the men and women, and then drew careful lines in the dust with their toes. Horses came to the watering troughs and nuzzled the water to clear the surface dust. After a while the faces of the watching men lost their bemused perplexity and became hard and angry and resistant. Then the women knew that they were safe and that there was no break. Then they asked, What'll we do? And the men replied, I don't know. But it was all right. The women knew it was all right, and the watching children knew it was all right. Women and children knew deep in themselves that no misfortune was too great to bear if their men were whole. The women went into the houses to their work, and the children began to play, but cautiously at first. As the day went forward the sun became less red. It flared down on the dust-blanketed land. The men sat in the doorways of their houses; their hands were busy with sticks and little rocks. The men sat still—thinking—figuring.

JOHN STEINBECK
The Grapes of Wrath, 1939

A Chronology of the Novel

Samuel Richardson, a prosperous printer and some-time scribe, completes *Pamela*, the first true novel; first circulating library opens in London

Henry Fielding begins long and fruitful career with *Shamela*, a parody that Richardson labels a "lewd and ungenerous engraftment" upon his *Pamela*

Fielding's second parody of the epistolary novel evolves into the wholly original *Joseph Andrews*

Pamela, printed in Philadelphia by Benjamin Franklin, becomes first novel published in America

Richardson answers critics and delights followers with his million-word masterpiece, *Clarissa;* Tobias Smollett, a Scottish surgeon, releases his first novel, the picaresque *Roderick Random*

Fielding finishes his ribald epic, *Tom Jones*, later described as the most perfectly plotted novel

Eccentric Irish clergyman Laurence Sterne publishes *Tristram Shandy*

With release of Horace Walpole's *The Castle of Otranto* the Gothic novel is born

In the year of his death Smollett completes *Humphry Clinker*, a brilliant fusion of the epistolary and picaresque novel forms

Les Liaisons dangereuses, sole novel of Choderlos de Laclos, a study of evil in epistolary form

Walter Scott, an Edinburgh lawyer, acquires Abbotsford, the vast Gothic mansion in which he writes thirty-one immensely popular historical romances; William Makepeace Thackeray born

The finely wrought novels of Jane Austen, the first consummate English novelist, begin to reach an avid audience; *Sense and Sensibility* and *Pride and Prejudice* are published shortly before her death in 1816, *Persuasion* and *Northanger Abbey* posthumously

Mary Wollstonecraft Shelley's first novel, *Frankenstein*, creates a sensation in literary London

Italian writer Alessandro Manzoni produces his multivolume historical novel, *The Betrothed*

The Leatherstocking Tales establish James Fenimore Cooper as the first great chronicler of the American frontier

Charles Dickens's *Pickwick Papers* marks debut of the most popular novelist of all time

Alexander Pushkin, greatest Russian poet and first major Russian short story writer, killed in a duel

Dickens's great serialized novels appear: *Oliver Twist* (1837–38), *Nicholas Nickelby* (1838–39), and *The Old Curiosity Shop* (1840–41)

Henri Beyle writes *The Charterhouse of Parma* under the pseudonym Stendhal

1740	War of the Austrian Succession embroils Europe in major conflict
1741	Handel completes his most famous oratorio, *Messiah*
1742	
1744	William Hogarth undertakes series of engravings entitled *Marriage à la Mode*
1748	Montesquieu publishes *Spirit of the Laws*
1749	
1755	Earthquake devastates Lisbon
1760-67	
1764	James Hargreaves invents the spinning jenny
1769	James Watt patents the steam engine
1771	
1776	American Declaration of Independence; publication of Adam Smith's *The Wealth of Nations*
1782	Rama I founds Chakin dynasty in Thailand, that still rules today
1785	*The Times* of London founded by John Walter; publication of Boswell's *Life of Samuel Johnson*
1789	Parisians storm the Bastille; Declaration of the Rights of Man proclaimed
1811	Paraguay wins independence from Spain
1811-18	
1812-14	The War of 1812; British burn Washington, D.C.
1815	Napoleon defeated at Waterloo
1818	
1821-27	
1823-27	
1836	Gogol's satiric comedy *The Inspector General* performed at court theater before Tsar Nicholas I
1837	Accession of Queen Victoria of England
1837-41	
1839	Outbreak of Opium War between Britain and China

Pushkin's fate befalls his most distinguished disciple, Mikhail Lermontov, who is killed in a duel one year after he finishes *A Hero of Our Time*; with "The Murders in the Rue Morgue" Edgar Allan Poe invents the detective story	1841	First production of the Romantic ballet *Giselle*; Dr. David Livingstone begins famous explorations in Africa
Dickens's maiden tour of the United States; Honoré de Balzac issues the first of seventy-odd volumes on life in nineteenth-century France, works known collectively as *La Comédie humaine*; initial installment of Nikolai Gogol's *Dead Souls*	1842	
A Christmas Carol, the most popular of all Dickens's works, is published	1843	
The Three Musketeers, The Count of Monte Cristo, and *Twenty Years After* written by Alexandre Dumas *père*, whose illegitimate son is chiefly remembered for his first novel, *La Dame aux Camélias* (1848)	1844-45	
A curious little volume entitled *Poems by Currer, Ellis, and Acton Bell*—the handiwork of Charlotte, Emily, and Anne Brontë—is released	1846	The Smithsonian Institution established by United States Congress
In a single, remarkably productive year, each of the Brontës completes a novel: Charlotte, *The Professor*; Anne, *Agnes Grey*; Emily, *Wuthering Heights*; Thackeray's *Vanity Fair* serialized	1847	
	1848	Revolutionary movements erupt and are quelled throughout Europe
Anne, Emily, and their brother Branwell Brontë die within eighteen months of one another	1848-49	
Publication of *The Scarlet Letter* brings immediate fame to Nathaniel Hawthorne; Dickens completes the heavily autobiographical *David Copperfield*	1850	United States Congress passes Compromise of 1850, an attempt to balance the nation's slavery and antislavery interests
Moby Dick, which its author, Herman Melville, describes as "broiled in hell fire," enjoys scant initial success; *Uncle Tom's Cabin*, by Harriet Beecher Stowe, directly influences the course of American political history	1851	London's Great Exhibition displays prosperity of life in Victorian England
Charlotte, the sole surviving Brontë, marries a clergyman, settles in London, and dies abruptly	1854	Outbreak of the Crimean War; Commodore Perry opens Japan to Western trade
Gustave Flaubert's search for "*le mot juste*" reaches its happy culmination with *Madame Bovary*	1856	
Mary Ann Evans releases *Scenes of Clerical Life* under the pseudonym George Eliot	1858	
Ivan Goncharov's plotless novel, *Oblomov*, issued	1859	French engineer Ferdinand de Lesseps initiates construction of Suez Canal
	1861-65	The American Civil War
Les Misérables, last major novel by Victor Hugo, the grand old man of French letters; Ivan Turgenev, the most cosmopolitan of Russian writers, completes *Fathers and Sons*	1862	The Mighty Five—Russian composers Balakirev, Cui, Borodin, Rimsky-Korsakov, and Moussorgsky—form a group dedicated to Russian national music
Leo Tolstoy's *War and Peace*, the supreme achievement in Russian fiction	1863-69	
Notes from Underground, first major work of Fyodor Dostoevsky	1864	
	1867	Alfred Nobel first manufactures dynamite
A Tale of Two Cities (1859), *Great Expectations* (1860–61), and *Our Mutual Friend* (1864–65) precede Dickens's final, triumphant tour of the United States	1867-68	
Dickens's premature death at the age of fifty-eight attributed to his taxing speaking schedule	1870	Lenin is born; outbreak of Franco-Prussian War
Emile Zola's twenty Rougon-Macquart novels—a latterday *Comédie humaine*—trace one family through several generations	1871-93	
George Eliot finishes *Middlemarch*, which Virginia Woolf later calls "one of the few English novels written for adult people"	1872	Dance impresario Sergei Diaghilev is born
Anna Karenina is Tolstoy's last major work before his religious conversion	1873-77	
	1874	First major exhibit of Impressionist paintings held in Paris

Guy de Maupassant's tales of the Franco-Prussian War mark Flaubert's former apprentice as master of the short story	1881-82
Dostoevsky's *The Brothers Karamazov* released shortly before his death; like *Crime and Punishment* and *The Idiot*, it focuses on violent crime	1881 Italian choreographer Luigi Manzotti stages *Excelsior*, a ballet extravaganza
Four years after leaving his post at *The Atlantic Monthly*, William Dean Howells publishes *The Rise of Silas Lapham*; Samuel Langhorne Clemens (Mark Twain) completes his American classic, *The Adventures of Huckleberry Finn*	1885 The Berlin Conference; Karl Benz and Gottlieb Daimler build the first automobile powered by an internal combustion engine
J'accuse, Zola's examination of the Dreyfus affair, marks him as a powerful polemicist	1894 Modern dance choreographer Martha Graham is born
The Red Badge of Courage, a fictionalized account of the 1863 battle of Chancellorsville, written by Stephen Crane, a young newspaperman who has never been to war	1895 Wilhelm Roentgen discovers X-rays; Lumière brothers open their Cinematographe
Jude the Obscure, last of Thomas Hardy's "Wessex" novels, a series that includes *The Return of the Native* (1878), *The Mayor of Casterbridge* (1886), and *Tess of the D'Urbervilles* (1891)	1896 First staging of Anton Chekhov's *The Seagull*
English journalist and social critic H.G. Wells publishes *The War of the Worlds*, a classic of the science fiction genre	1898 Founding of the Moscow Art Theatre by Stanislavsky and Nemirovich-Danchenko; production of George Bernard Shaw's *Candida*
Theodore Dreiser's *Sister Carrie* released by its publisher, Doubleday, Page; Joseph Conrad's masterpiece, *Lord Jim*, completed	1900 Founding of the Labour Party in Great Britain; Boxer Rebellion crushed in China
The novels of Henry James's major phase: *The Wings of the Dove*, *The Ambassadors*, *The Golden Bowl*	1902-04
Death of Anton Chekhov, acknowledged master of the Russian short story; Vanessa and Virginia Stephen settle in Bloomsbury section of London, become nucleus of coterie that includes Clive Bell (who marries Vanessa), Leonard Woolf (who marries Virginia), T.S. Eliot, Lytton Strachey, E.M. Forster	1904 Moscow Art Theatre produces Chekhov's final play, *The Cherry Orchard*
Publication of *The Man of Property*, first in John Galsworthy's nine-novel series, *The Forsyte Saga*	1906
Arnold Bennett, who stands alongside Galsworthy as a narrator of upper-middle-class English mores, publishes *The Old Wives' Tale*, his finest work	1908 Kandinsky's works mark the beginning of abstract art
André Gide founds *La Nouvelle Revue Française*, which becomes the nation's most influential literary magazine, and publishes his first novel	1909 Expedition led by Robert E. Peary reaches the North Pole
	1914 Outbreak of World War I
D.H. Lawrence's *The Rainbow* briefly suppressed by the censors who are to plague the author throughout his career	1915 Release of D.W. Griffith's *The Birth of a Nation*
Marcel Proust's *Remembrance of Things Past*, the seven-volume "culmination" of the French novel, offers an intensely personal portrait of a society doomed to extinction by World War I	1917-27
Willa Cather's *My Ántonia* provides an enduring portrait of life on the American prairie during the late nineteenth century	1918 Republic proclaimed in Germany; Communist revolt in Hungary organized by Bela Kun
Sherwood Anderson's haunting, influential *Winesburg, Ohio* released	1919 Treaty of Versailles ends World War I
Publication in Paris of James Joyce's landmark novel, *Ulysses*	1922 Establishment of the Irish Free State
Corydon, Gide's defense of homosexuality, scandalizes Paris; author flees to French Equatorial Africa; he is still in exile when *The Counterfeiters* is released two years later; E.M. Forster's study of English colonial rule in India, *A Passage to India*, published; Thomas Mann's *The Magic Mountain* written in the traditional German novel form, the *Bildungsroman*	1924 First performance of Gershwin's *Rhapsody in Blue*; André Breton publishes manifesto on Surrealism
Virginia Woolf publishes her finest works: *Mrs. Dalloway* (1925), *To the Lighthouse* (1927), *The Waves* (1931)	1925-31

An American Tragedy represents the culmination of Dreiser's career as destroyer of the "genteel tradition" in American prose fiction; F. Scott Fitzgerald's quintessential narrative of the Jazz Age, *The Great Gatsby*; Franz Kafka's *The Trial* published posthumously by his friend Max Brod

Reputation of Ernest Hemingway established following publication of *The Sun Also Rises*

Thomas Wolfe's *Look Homeward, Angel*, a great success; the South emerges as a rich source of American literature in such works as William Faulkner's *The Sound and the Fury*

United States Supreme Court rules *Ulysses* is not obscene and allows its sale in the U.S.

The hardships of life during the Depression form the background for John Steinbeck's Pulitzer Prize-winning novel, *The Grapes of Wrath*

Virginia Woolf commits suicide

Albert Camus publishes *The Stranger*, a novel written while he was a journalist in North Africa

French novelist Colette becomes first woman inducted into the prestigious Goncourt Academy

Norman Mailer completes *The Naked and the Dead*, finest novel written about World War II

Ralph Ellison's *Invisible Man* explores the problems of blacks living in a white society

Chicago-based author Saul Bellow gains national prominence following success of *The Adventures of Augie March*

English translation of Boris Pasternak's *Doctor Zhivago*; Pasternak awarded Nobel Prize for literature, but Soviet pressure forces him to decline the honor

Doris Lessing's *The Golden Notebook* explores woman's role in modern society

One Hundred Years of Solitude by Gabriel García Márquez, a major Spanish-language work

Alexander Solzhenitsyn's *The First Circle* published outside the Soviet Union; two years later Solzhenitsyn awarded Nobel Prize for literature

Solzhenitsyn forced into exile by Soviet authorities following release of his nonfiction account of Russian prison life, *The Gulag Archipelago*

1925	Death of Sun Yat-sen, the father of the Republic of China; Sergei Eisenstein directs *Potemkin*
1926	Rioting in Dublin follows performance of O'Casey's *The Plough and the Stars* at the Abbey Theatre
1929	Stock market crash on Wall Street leads to worldwide economic depression
1933	Adolf Hitler becomes chancellor of Germany; Franklin D. Roosevelt takes oath as thirty-second President of the United States
1939	German invasion of Poland marks beginning of World War II
1941	Japanese attack Pearl Harbor; the United States enters the war
1942	Enrico Fermi creates the first self-sustaining nuclear chain reaction
1945	Allies defeat Germany; the first atomic bombs are used against Japan to end World War II in the Pacific
1948	Creation of the state of Israel
1952	Gamal Abdal Nasser leads army coup to overthrow Egyptian monarchy
1953	Death of Stalin; armistice is signed in Korea
1958	Mies van der Rohe's Seagram Building completed
1962	Cuban missile crisis; Pope John XXIII opens the Second Vatican Council
1967	Arab-Israeli Six-Day War; first human heart transplant performed by Dr. Christiaan Barnard
1968	Russian troops invade Czechoslovakia to stifle liberal regime of Alexander Dubcek
1974	President Nixon, facing impeachment over Watergate scandal, resigns

One Hundred Great Novels

Every serious reader has his own list of favorite novels, a compilation as idiosyncratic as that reader's tastes and as boundless as his enthusiasm. Although such lists often tally closely, they rarely overlap completely—and the following compendium is in no way meant to be definitive. It simply sets forth, in chronological order within each subdivision, the authors and titles of one hundred recognized classics of the novelist's art.

BRITISH

Daniel Defoe, *Moll Flanders*
Samuel Richardson, *Clarissa*
Henry Fielding, *Joseph Andrews* and *Tom Jones*
Tobias Smollett, *Humphry Clinker*
Laurence Sterne, *Tristram Shandy*
Sir Walter Scott, *The Heart of Midlothian*
Jane Austen, *Pride and Prejudice* and *Emma*
Charles Dickens, *Bleak House* and *Great Expectations*
Charlotte Brontë, *Jane Eyre*
Emily Brontë, *Wuthering Heights*
William Thackeray, *Vanity Fair*
George Eliot, *The Mill on the Floss* and *Middlemarch*
Anthony Trollope, *Barchester Towers*
Thomas Hardy, *Tess of the D'Urbervilles*
    Jude the Obscure
George Meredith, *The Egoist*
Samuel Butler, *The Way of All Flesh*
Joseph Conrad, *Lord Jim* and *Nostromo*
Max Beerbohm, *Zuleika Dobson*
Ford Madox Ford, *The Good Soldier*
John Galsworthy, *The Forsyte Saga*
Arnold Bennett, *The Old Wives' Tale*
H. G. Wells, *Tono-Bungay*
D. H. Lawrence, *Sons and Lovers* and *The Rainbow*
James Joyce, *A Portrait of the Artist as a Young Man*
    Ulysses
Virginia Woolf, *Mrs. Dalloway* and *To the Lighthouse*
E. M. Forster, *A Passage to India*
Aldous Huxley, *Point Counter Point*
Evelyn Waugh, *A Handful of Dust*
Lawrence Durrell, *The Alexandria Quartet*
Anthony Powell, *A Dance to the Music of Time*
George Orwell, *1984*

AMERICAN

Nathaniel Hawthorne, *The Scarlet Letter*
Herman Melville, *Moby Dick*
Mark Twain, *The Adventures of Huckleberry Finn*
Henry James, *The Portrait of a Lady*
    The Ambassadors
William Dean Howells, *The Rise of Silas Lapham*
Stephen Crane, *The Red Badge of Courage*
Theodore Dreiser, *Sister Carrie* and *An American Tragedy*
Edith Wharton, *The Age of Innocence*
Willa Cather, *My Antonia*
Sinclair Lewis, *Babbitt*
F. Scott Fitzgerald, *The Great Gatsby*
    Tender Is the Night

Ernest Hemingway, *The Sun Also Rises*
    A Farewell to Arms
William Faulkner, *The Sound and the Fury*
    Light in August
Thomas Wolfe, *Look Homeward, Angel*
John Steinbeck, *The Grapes of Wrath*
John Dos Passos, *U.S.A.*

FRENCH

Choderlos de Laclos, *Les Liaisons dangereuses*
Stendhal, *The Red and the Black*
    The Charterhouse of Parma
Honoré de Balzac, *Père Goriot* and *Lost Illusions*
Gustave Flaubert, *Madame Bovary*
    The Sentimental Education
Voltaire, *Candide*
Victor Hugo, *Les Misérables*
Emile Zola, *Germinal*
Marcel Proust, *Remembrance of Things Past*
André Gide, *The Counterfeiters*
André Malraux, *Man's Fate*
Henry de Montherlant, *The Bachelors*
Albert Camus, *The Plague*

RUSSIAN

Mikhail Lermontov, *A Hero of Our Time*
Nikolai Gogol, *Dead Souls*
Ivan Goncharov, *Oblomov*
Fyodor Dostoevsky, *Crime and Punishment*
    The Brothers Karamazov
Ivan Turgenev, *Fathers and Sons*
Leo Tolstoy, *War and Peace* and *Anna Karenina*
Boris Pasternak, *Doctor Zhivago*
Alexander Solzhenitsyn, *The First Circle*

OTHER

Lady Murasaki, *The Tale of Genji*
Junichiro Tanizaki, *The Makioka Sisters*
Johann von Goethe, *The Sorrows of Young Werther*
Thomas Mann, *Buddenbrooks* and *The Magic Mountain*
Franz Kafka, *The Trial*
Robert Musil, *The Man Without Qualities*
Günter Grass, *The Tin Drum*
Sigrid Undset, *Kristin Lavransdatter*
O. E. Rölvaag, *Giants in the Earth*
Miguel de Cervantes Saavedra, *Don Quixote*
Alessandro Manzoni, *The Betrothed*
Italo Svevo, *The Confessions of Zeno*
Ignazio Silone, *Bread and Wine*

Selected Bibliography

Allen, Walter. *The English Novel*. New York: Dutton, 1955.

Bennett, E. K. *A History of the German Novelle*. Cambridge: Cambridge University Press, 1965.

Bewley, Marius. *The Eccentric Design: Form in the Classic American Novel*. New York: Columbia University Press, 1963.

Booth, Wayne C. *The Rhetoric of Fiction*. Chicago: University of Chicago Press, 1961.

Chase, Richard. *The American Novel and Its Tradition*. New York: Doubleday, 1957.

Drew, Elizabeth. *The Novel*. New York: Dell, 1963.

Forster, E. M. *Aspects of the Novel*. New York: Harcourt Brace Jovanovich, 1927.

Franco, Jean. *An Introduction to Spanish American Literature*. Cambridge: Cambridge University Press, 1969.

Harss, Luis and Dohmann, Barbara. *Into the Mainstream*. New York: Harper & Row, 1969.

Kazin, Alfred. *On Native Grounds*. New York: Harcourt Brace Jovanovich, 1942.

Kettle, Arnold. *An Introduction to the English Novel*. 2 vols. New York: Harper & Row, 1960.

Leavis, F. R. *The Great Tradition*. London: Chatto and Windus, 1962.

Lubbock, Percy. *The Craft of Fiction*. New York: Viking Press, 1957.

Mirsky, D. S. *A History of Russian Literature*. New York: Vintage, 1958.

Muchnic, Helen. *An Introduction to Russian Literature*. New York: Dutton, 1964.

Muir, Edwin. *The Structure of the Novel*. London: The Hogarth Press, 1954.

Neill, S. D. *A Short History of the English Novel*. New York: Macmillan, 1952.

Pacifici, Sergio. *The Modern Italian Novel, from Manzoni to Svevo*. Carbondale: Southern Illinois University Press, 1967.

Pritchett, V. S. *The Living Novel and Later Appreciations*. New York: Vintage, 1967.

Rathburn, Robert C. and Steinmann, Martin Jr., ed. *From Jane Austen to Joseph Conrad*. Minneapolis: University of Minnesota Press, 1958.

Simmons, Ernest J. *Introduction to Russian Realism*. Bloomington: Indiana University Press, 1965.

Tillotson, Kathleen. *Novels of the Eighteen-Forties*. New York: Oxford University Press, 1954.

Turnell, Martin. *The Novel in France*. New York: Vintage, 1951.

Van Ghent, Dorothy. *The English Novel: Form and Function*. New York: Holt, Rinehart and Winston, 1953.

Zabel, Morton Dauwen. *Craft and Character in Modern Fiction*. New York: Viking Press, 1957.

Picture Credits

The Editors would like to thank the following for their assistance:
Russell Ash, London
E. Norman Flayderman, New Milford, Connecticut
Barbara Nagelsmith, Paris
National Gallery of Art, Washington—Kathleen Kissane
New York Public Library, Berg Collection—Dr. Lola Szladits, David Pankow
New York Public Library, Rare Book Division—Maud Cole
New-York Historical Society—Wilson Duprey

The following abbreviations are used:
BNP —Bibliothèque Nationale, Paris
(BB) —(Brown Brothers)
(CP) —(Culver Pictures)
(M) —(Mondadori Archives)
NPG —National Portrait Gallery, London
(N) —(Newsweek Archives)
NYPL—New York Public Library

HALF TITLE Symbol by Jay J. Smith Studio FRONTISPIECE (Anthony Howarth)

CHAPTER 1 **6** By Gracious Permission of Her Majesty Elizabeth II, Windsor Castle **8** Rare Book Division, NYPL **10** Both: British Museum **11** NPG **12** & **13** Astor, Lenox & Tilden Foundations, NYPL **14** All: NYPL **15** British

Index